The World of the Gifted Child

The
World
of the
Gifted Child

Priscilla L. Vail

WALKER AND COMPANY
NEW YORK

First published in the United States of America in 1979 by the Walker Publishing Company, Inc.

Published simultaneously in Canada by Beaverbooks, Limited, Pickering, Ontario.

ISBN: 0-8027-0611-8

Library of Congress Catalog Card Number: 78-58598

Printed in the United States of America

10 9 8 7 6 5 4 3 2

To
      Donald
and our children
      Melissa, Polly, Lucia, and Angus

"I would rather learn from one bird how to sing
Than teach ten thousand stars how not to dance."

e.e. cummings

Acknowledgments

My thanks go to all the people who, individually and through their organizations, have helped me write this book. Sometimes gourmet cooks will pretend to give you their recipes while actually leaving out vital ingredients. Not so my friends who have generously shared their insights, practical knowledge, understanding, and time.

Margaret Mayo-Smith, Charlotte Goodhue, Anne and John Zinsser, and a legion of Lukes have given me courage, criticism, and copy.

Waldo Jones, head of our lower school, and Sam Parkman, our headmaster, are wise educators and treasured friends. I am grateful to them, my colleagues at Rippowam-Cisqua, and the children, all of whom have been my teachers.

The National Association of Independent Schools has always championed the cause of gifted children, explicitly and implicitly. Through their conferences, and their magazine *Independent School*, they reach a tremendous number of educators, and are always willing to take a strong philosophical stand. I am grateful to them for having been the first to publish the article that appears as the basis of Chapter One of this book and for exploring the question of language development in their publications and their meetings. Special recognition is due to Blair McElroy, an editor of superhu-

Acknowledgments

man ability and warmth, and Gordon Clem, quiet guardian of childhood.

The Orton Society sheds the light of understanding on the problems of language-disabled children. I have learned so much at Orton conferences and was proud to present some of the ideas in Chapter Eight at their World Conference on Dyslexia in Dallas, Texas, in November, 1977, under the title *Limerence; Language Literature and Listening.* I give special thanks to Aylett R. Cox, a wise, humorous, and articulate teacher; Alice Ansara, an editor who gives her time and intellectual energy without reserve, and Katrina de Hirsch and Jeannette Jansky, who have built a beacon with their work.

I am grateful and proud that Henry Collis, director of the National Association for Gifted Children in London, was willing to vault the Atlantic Ocean and write the foreword for this book. Such a feat is no surprise considering his soaring mind, limitless agility, and his ties with Jane Burditt and Lucy Stanton, who, as Educator's Ally, Inc., in Bedford, New York, plan conferences, arrange meetings, and spread the word.

To Elizabeth Bauserman go my thanks for seemingly infinite amounts of patience and perfect typing.

A toast to two wizards of words: Edward Streeter, author, tease, and mentor, and my editor Richard Winslow at Walker, who, were he listed under W, might be described: wise, willing, wonderful —wry and rarely wrong.

Priscilla L. Vail
August, 1978

Foreword

In contrast to the tired and sometimes jealous jargon which hits the headlines in describing gifted children, this book is a balanced testament of sound common sense. The author is fortunate to have been able to write with one eye on the growing processes of her own gifted daughter, but this has not in any way narrowed her vision to the development of one child. The view is wide, the findings sound, and the observations meaningful. In short, we have here an amalgam of varied information as valuable to parents as to teachers and well worth reading by anybody interested in children.

It is good very early on to meet Lucia's sense of humor, for here is the saving grace of many a clever child. In a crisis the lighter touch can prove the finest aid to evasive action, as I found myself many times when I was a headmaster. If a child was brave and witty enough to try to lower the temperature by not being as serious as the situation seemed to demand, I invariably succumbed. It is not a question of being impertinent but can illustrate the insight given to socially gifted children to see through the adult glare and dig down into the friendliness which should always be on call.

This deep understanding of themselves and of what other people are really thinking is a characteristic which becomes very marked as gifted children tackle the dark ages of adolescence. Their problems can be deep seated and call for endless patience. How fully I agree with the author in the way she expresses this. And how wrong the world can be in its ready opinion of children in their formative years—the terror (not insolence) that can bring a laugh at the wrong moment, the eagerness to help a teacher that is a cry for companionship and not an attempt to curry favor, the brilliant child who is three or four years ahead intellectually but far behind emotionally. How easy for those who do not understand to regard the child as an uncomfortable freak whose lopsided development is beyond repair. As this book makes so very clear, gifted children are human beings and must be given every chance to grow up physically, emotionally, intellectually, and socially. Then they can lead balanced lives, at ease in the company of people with normal intelligence, yet finding scope in their work to reach a potential which can make a very powerful contribution.

At home, it is not an easy task to see the end product when facing sleepless nights, defiance in face of correction, and the aloofness of total withdrawal. But when reading this book, parents can take great comfort from what can emerge when parents are patient and tolerant, almost at times to the breaking point. The British National Association for Gifted Children has had unique opportunities since 1966 of glimpsing homes and their problems. Every week parents write and give accounts quite similar to those you will read about, only more of ours come from deprived families. Some of these parents view the prospect of having a brilliant child with apprehension and incredulity. This is taken straight from one letter I had: "We don't know if his development is in any way unusual, but by 2¼ his vocabulary was over 500 words and by 2½ over 900, at 3½ he used words like 'swivel, dissolve, muscle and shipshape.' So agile that the fence has been reinforced several times and the garden looks like a detention centre. So inquisitive that all drawers within reach have been tied up with string for two years. So determined that he regards any form of direct control as a challenge and then it is like coming up against a reinforced concrete wall. So observant that at 2½ he picked up half a biscuit and said 'that's a semi-circle' and then half a sandwich and said 'that's a triangle.' Can you help us decide whether this is a perfectly normal little boy?"

What is most important, and this is well brought out in Part II, "How They Live," is that gifted children must feel that they are wanted and that they are loved like their brother and sister. They are particularly in need of cuddling when small, of a great deal of talking to before they speak, and of being gently helped to develop as fast as nature makes easily possible. To force a child because a parent may be obsessed with an unfulfilled ambition of his own is just as bad as to hold a child back so as to make him conform. This latter trait must seem strange to Americans, but I do occasionally run across parents in poor areas who regard it as a stigma to have an intellectually gifted child. They fear there will be bullying at school and jeers from the neighbours. The easiest solution seems to be to try to make him appear less brainy and more average. My experience therefore bears out entirely the vulnerability of some parents which is implicit in this chapter.

Parents are often perplexed by the way their children become obsessed with some idea or some problem and will withdraw utterly into themselves and concentrate for hours on end. They are consumed with a burning interest which nothing should interrupt. However, at school a few hours later they may switch off entirely, like electric light, because of lack of rapport with the teacher. Burning zeal has given way to restless frustration. How very right, then, Priscilla Vail is to give top priority to the need at school for a "goodness of fit" (in that telling phrase by Herbert Birch). If a gifted child feels at home in his classroom, relates well

xi

to his teacher, and is given demanding enough work he can be an inspiration to teach and an exciting challenge to his peers.

But there is only a hairline between high endeavor and depressing languor. On this point many useful individual case histories are quoted and much sound advice is given, but the overriding factor is that parents must be in harmony with the school. If they find this is impossible because their child is showing none of the zest they see at home, they must somehow be loyal to the school in front of the child or say nothing. In approaching the school they must remember they never see Johnnie when they are not there, and that children can behave very differently away from home. Before criticizing the teacher they must be frank with themselves and ask whether the root cause is in fact too much pressure at home or too much questioning on the school day and then putting too much credence on the stories they are told, perhaps touched up with lurid elaborations of any self-respecting imagination. Gifted children are intensely sensitive to prying and many collisions occur between parent and teacher because it is not accepted at home that, just as Father is not pestered with questions about the office, so should Junior not be bothered overmuch about how his day has gone at school.

Most teachers try to help each child according to his ability but gifted children whom they cannot motivate are a plain nuisance, specially if they are immature socially. Without the comparison of other children, parents may not realize and just clamor for acceleration. Occasionally a teacher driven to distraction bursts out with a condemnation of the work done as proof the child is *not* gifted. This can well be a false assumption because achievement and potential do not always go in double harness. Or teacher and parent may have overlooked that the child has a shortness of auditory attention which is leading to various problems. He cannot easily listen to what is said and will be worse off still if there is the background noise which is almost unavoidable in many school situations.

The problems that can be encountered at school and at home come out many times in this book, which also stresses the joy which the majority of gifted children can bring to those they meet. Their zest and sparkle can embellish their surroundings. They love life and life loves them. That is the happy message which predominates, but we must also take to heart the poignant passages, for these tell of gifted children in need. It is easy to forget in making generalizations that with every child, gifted or otherwise, the most telling factors in his life are the horizon and the climate which surround him when he is in his desk at school.

Whatever money is allocated from the Office of Education in Washington to meet the needs of gifted children, whatever enrichment programs are arranged locally, whatever well-intentioned teachers talk about at conferences, whatever far-reaching research is undertaken, nothing avails unless the child himself is able to thrive in his own personal school world. If there is fear or frustration, is the system at fault or could it be the failing of one teacher?

I have heard cynics say, "Why help gifted children? They have everything" or "Why not look after the slow learners and leave those lucky ones to teach themselves?" If all gifted children were mature, placid, evenly balanced intellectually, and socially adjusted, this could often happen to a reasonable degree, although few would reach their full potential. Unfortunately, some of these children are bewildered and have anything but a robust outlook. They are extremely sensitive and painfully allergic to sarcasm or feeling that they are in the way. Let an eleven-year-old boy whom I know well describe in his words what happened to him. He called his poem *The Wall*.

FOREWORD

They laughed at me.
They laughed at me and called me names,
They wouldn't let me join their games.
I couldn't understand.
I spent most playtimes on my own,
Everywhere I was alone,
I couldn't understand.

Teachers told me I was rude,
Bumptious, over-bearing, shrewd,
Some of the things they said were crude.
I couldn't understand.
And so I built myself a wall.
Strong and solid, ten foot tall,
With bricks you couldn't see at all,
So *I* could understand.

And then came Sir,
A jovial, beaming, kindly man,
Saw through my wall and took my hand,
And the bricks came tumbling down,
For *he* could understand.

And now I laugh with them,
Not in any unkind way,
For they have yet to face their day
And the lessons I have learned.
For eagles soar above all birds,
And scavengers need to hunt in herds,
But the lion walks alone,
And now I understand.

We can understand too a great deal better when we have digested the recipes for success which Priscilla Vail so deftly sets out. Are there still teachers so out of touch with modern thinking that they are unsympathetic to children who are gifted? If they exist let other faculty members gently nudge *The World of the Gifted Child* their way with a muttered, "Well, there is a book which *you* won't read."

Who knows? It may quietly vanish from the faculty library and perhaps in a few weeks' time there are signs that the ranks of those like "Sir" in the poem are happily reinforced. One teacher has become much wiser. Gifted children need no longer dread his coming. There is now a goodness of fit.

Henry Collis
July, 1978

Contents

Prologue

This book is born of a combination of past experience, current concern, and hope for the future of gifted children.

As each child is a gift, so each child comes with distinguishing gifts. For some, the balance makes for a tranquil passage through life. For others, the balance produces frustrations, dreams, and energies which resemble the tides of the sea in their power and relentlessness.

Giftedness brings its own particular set of pleasures and perils. My husband and I have learned about some of them through our own family life. As a teacher and a parent I want to share what insights I have with others who are concerned with children: educators, parents, physicians, those who plan community projects, and enlightened caretakers who want to protect and support gifted children so they may grow into whole people.

Gifted children have intense emotional and social needs that are frequently sacrificed to intellectual or academic concerns, particularly when educators get into the act. Being a teacher myself, I feel a license to criticize my own profession which I might deny to an outsider.

PROLOGUE

My current worry is that as giftedness nudges other special educational needs aside in the popular and professional press, two things are happening. The first is a denigrating of the needs of gifted children. This springs from a philosophical discomfort with the idea of favoritism for an endowed elite. We prize equality so highly that superlative performance is often suspect. Paradoxically this coexists with ready applause for superheroes in sports, moneymaking and daredeviling. The idea of singling out one element of the population for special support is mistrusted unless the element is below the average. It is idealistically comfortable to help the underdog. Topdog is supposed to take care of himself.

The second cause for my concern is the limelight recently thrown on a group of children labeled "the gifted and talented." Suddenly these children are the focus of a great deal of governmental and professional attention. Their lives will be microscopically examined, they will be the objects of studies, and the recipients of hot, new, educational materials. This may be wonderful, or it may not. It all depends on whether the live child is found in the program or sacrificed to it.

In order to understand how we can best nurture gifted children, we first need to know who they are and how we can recognize them. Then we must see how they live, within their families, with their friends, and in their world, and what role school plays in their lives. We can then consider what additional nourishment they need. Finally, we can look at the lives of nine gifted people, five male and four female, who range in age from six to seventy-five, and listen to their words and wishes.

I intentionally blur the boundaries between genius, prodigy, gifted child, and bright kid because, even using the most sophisticated available diagnostic instrument, I'm not sure it is possible to make accurate distinctions, particularly when the children are young. Chapter Two will take up this question in greater detail. Although the philosophy and suggestions in this book were written primarily about gifted children, there is nothing here to harm a child who might be more accurately described as able or bright.

Each time my life has been touched by the people who appear on these pages I have received a gift.

PART I

Who They Are

Chapter 1

Lucia's Story

The first thing we have to remember about gifted children is that they are children. Like other children, they grow, lose their baby teeth, cry, laugh, and suffer the glories and pains of growing up. People are sometimes intimidated by their intelligence and think that just because they have giant vocabularies or understand quadratic equations they have the world by the tail. Not so.

Our gifted child introduced us to the wonders and problems of her life. As my husband and I—and her schools—tried to provide the best possible environment for her, we learned a lot about all gifted children. We learned from the good choices we made when we used our common sense; and more important, we learned from our mistakes. We learned why some current theories about educating the gifted don't have much to do with live children.

Lucia was the third of three daughters born to us at two-year intervals. She was an impatient baby, eager to be rid of the trappings of infancy. She hated being in a buggy or a basket. While her disposition improved when she could sit up and see more, she was

3

frustrated until she could walk. Then, she had both vistas and independence, and she began to laugh.

She played with all of the usual household toys, and her early talking didn't seem unusual, given the constant companionship of her very verbal older sisters. In spite of this facility, she kept many of her thoughts and accomplishments to herself in a kind of emotional and intellectual privacy. She was a passionate small person with what seemed like quirkily adult ways of seeing the world.

She did ordinary nursery school things in nursery school and appeared to be doing the same in kindergarten. No one knew she could read until one spring morning when she announced to the class at playground that everyone would be having cupcakes and chocolate milk the next day. Queried on her source of information, she was stopped short. Having blown her cover, she had to admit that she had read it on the teacher's desk.

After recess, the teacher sat down with her to give her some other things to read, ranging from first-grade books through *The Wizard of Oz*. She could read them all with ease and comprehension. No one had taught her. She said she just knew how, and indeed she did.

The school found this extraordinary. We tried to play it down because, although our fourth-grade daughter was whizzing along academically, our second-grade daughter was having a devilish time learning to read and spell.

Summer came, with its puppets, costumes, bathing suits, picnics, and library cards. Lucia enjoyed them all and made the September journey to the shoe store with enthusiasm and excitement about entering first grade.

No more than two weeks had gone by before the school called to schedule an appointment right away. They came right to the point. There was no way they could keep Lucia in the first grade. She already knew all the work planned for the rest of the year, not only in reading, but in math and in general information and concepts. Her being so far ahead was demoralizing to the other children, and some parents had also complained. (In 1961, competition was rampant in rigorous schools. It involved class standing as well as marks, and it began as early as first grade.) Some parents argued that it wasn't fair for their children to have to compete with someone who already knew the material.

The teacher didn't feel she could keep Lucia. No, she wasn't making any trouble. She was cooperative and seemed glad to be there, but surely she would soon be bored, and discipline problems would follow.

We agreed that boredom is a threat to curiosity and that curiosity deserves protection. However, we wondered whether Lucia couldn't be given some projects to do while the group was working on skills she already had. We were told that this wasn't possible. It would be poor for classroom morale and discipline and would single her out and separate her from the group. (How strange this now sounds, given today's flexibility in many classrooms.)

What was to be done, then, with our cheery little misfit? The school suggested moving her forthwith into second grade. This raised many questions in our minds. Would she be accepted as a member of the class, joining them late, younger, and with some sort of favored status? Surely the kiss of death. Would second-grade work be right for her? She was already reading comfortably at third-grade level and above.

How much of a handicap would a full year's deficit be to Lucia in sports? Her athletic ability was only average for her own age, and sports are important for establishing a place in the group. What about always being a year younger than your classmates in terms of psychological development, activities, and boy-girl relationships?

We could see from our fifth grader that these concerns would be upon us in no time. The decision we made now would have to

5

carry us over more than just the next year. It would be foolish and harmful to sidestep a present problem if it meant putting up obstacles for the future.

The school acknowledged all these potential difficulties but recommended—insisted actually—that Lucia be moved on Monday. They felt they were dealing with an exceptional intellect that was in a period of vigorous growth. If they didn't stimulate her mind at such a moment, Lucia, with her passionate and purposeful nature, could be turned away from learning for life—something the school was unwilling to risk.

We were all thinking and trying hard up to this point. Then we all made a wrong assumption. "Because she is so smart," they said, "she will be able to figure out the social problems." We agreed.

Lucia went into second grade and, after some preliminary skirmishing, was fairly well accepted. Her classmates enjoyed her sense of humor and the stories and plays she made up. She was known in the group for being musical as well as smart. That seemed to take away some of the sting. She did well enough in sports, and the work was all right, even though it presented very little challenge. We didn't mind that because we were glad that she had enough physical and mental energy left at the end of the day for extracurricular and creative pursuits.

Lucia had smooth sailing through second, third, fourth and part of the fifth grade. Then the trouble began.

At first, it just seemed to be an energetic wave of showing off. Hoping it was a phase, we decided to ride it out. The school thought she had gotten too big for her britches and decided to crack down. Later, we and Lucia came to understand that all of a sudden, she saw her classmates moving away from her to some new level. She used her tried and true humor and song and dance routines to call them back to where she was. They, having reached a new level, saw her antics as a pain in the neck and drew even farther away. The problem got worse.

Sixth grade was really bad. Although she was doing excellent academic work, Lucia was friendless, rude, and seemingly uncaring. Moodiness, sarcasm, and antagonism were the order of the day. Her humorous tongue developed a deadly edge honed by practice. She was no joy to others and no joy to herself. Everyone was concerned.

That spring I went to hear the fifth and sixth grades sing. Music had remained a constant joy for Lucia. I looked at the sixth graders lined up on the stage—tall, faces growing in that bone-expanding way that heralds adolescence. Boys were getting thicker through the chest, and girls had bosoms. Then there was Lucia, flat of chest, delicate of face like—yes—like all the fifth graders.

I wondered whether she should be back with her contemporaries and shared my thoughts with the school. They said that, even though she was having a very bad time socially and emotionally, her academic work was excellent. The dangers of boredom were mentioned again, and I got the familiar, "A kid as smart as she is will figure all this social stuff out." We weren't convinced, and got their blessing to talk the idea over with Lucia.

We suggested a move, and her initial reaction (as it was to everything) was negative. We said that she might feel better being with people her own age, even though she was so good at her work. We told her honestly that the school was afraid she might get bored repeating a year, but that we didn't feel she was enjoying her work, or her life, very much. She didn't really seem to be getting much out of it except good marks.

Memorial Day weekend brought the imminence of final exams. Lucia's sisters did diligent things with Latin verbs and history dates. Lucia played with her hamster, stayed up late, and played the radio—loud. She failed four out of six exams and greeted the

7

news with a matter-of-fact, rather cheerful, "Well, I guess I'll have to stay back."

Her own age group accepted her more kindly than one might have expected. They all grew bosoms together. And, though she read the same stories and studied the same history as she had the year before, she brought such different perceptions to them that they seemed new.

New, also, was the experience of feeling a certain way about a character or event and finding that other people did, too. That had never happened to her in school before.

No matter how smart you are, you can't be twelve when you're eleven. You don't feel like a twelve-year-old when you're eleven. If you try, you're a fake twelve, and you miss being eleven. You have to go back later and pick up what you've missed, like a dropped stitch. The more rows you knit beyond the dropped stitch, the harder it is to weave it back up. That was Lucia's next task.

Lucia's high scores, high marks, and highest possible percentiles in standardized testing all gave the appearance of a brilliant child working at full capacity. Her great facility with words continued to help her learn quickly and easily from books.

Verbal expression—written, oral, and dramatic—was a happy outlet for her creative energies. It was tempting to encourage her to go on in these fields by fostering vertical growth in her strong area. But concentration on vertical growth is not what the gifted child needs.

Lucia graduated from elementary school at the end of ninth grade and went off for one year to an extremely demanding boarding school, which gave a surface appearance of individuality and creativity.

While showing us around, the headmaster said, "We have nothing here to force standardized behavior on our students—no uniforms, no one set of academic requirements. We have a community of individuals—all very different. Children this bright and this creative are free thinkers and enjoy being different from one another."

What he didn't say, and what we forgot, is that children of this age seek out kinds of conformity because they need the safety of a group code. It may appear in shared tastes for styles of dress, slang, or antagonisms, but it is part of every adolescent group.

When so much is shifting inside, the child needs visible, external confirmation that others are like him.[1] He already feels different and perhaps frighteningly alone. The world of adult support should provide ways for him to feel more connected, not more isolated.

When the adult world denies the existence and value of such conformity, it doesn't disappear. Instead, it goes underground, and the more subtle it is, the more rigid and binding its requirements, and thus the harder it is to discard or outgrow.

In Lucia's school, once again, adult expectations, based on assessment of intellectual capacity, worked to deny rather than enhance normal progression through developmental stages.

The head said, "Young people with this kind of intellect have different emotional needs from other young people. They are so quick to see, and to understand, that they are really much older than their chronological age. They don't need as much emotional support or time. They need more intellectual challenge."

Wrong. These children who are so quick to see patterns and grasp implications need even more chances to grow emotionally. Enhanced perception means enhanced perception of both pain and joy, not just joy, and of the discrepancy between how you see yourself and how the world sees you.

Bringing these two images into focus is one of the major tasks of growing up, as it is one of the manifestations of autonomy. Any time the trusted adult world reinforces the discrepancy in the two

---

[1] I use the masculine pronoun throughout the book because the constant use of "he or she" is cumbersome, and I wanted to settle on one. I flipped a coin.

9

images by ignoring or denying its existence, it makes pain for the child. Any time the trusted adult world can say, by implication or words, that "growing up is just as hard for you as it is for anyone else," it demonstrates acceptance and understanding from which the child can draw real support.

In this respect, dealing with the gifted is very like dealing with the learning-disabled. The learning-disabled child's bluffs and camouflages seem to say, "If they find out how bad I am at that, they won't like (or accept) me any more." The gifted child may be worrying, "If they find out that inside of me I'm not made of magic and excellence they won't like (or accept) me any more." The underlying question for both is, "If I'm not what they think I am, do I exist?"

One of the first tasks for a teacher who deals with a learning-disabled child is to acknowledge his disability while accepting him, simultaneously, as a person. We must treat our gifted students with the same understanding and acceptance.

Socially, the gifted child starts with an extra handicap. The world is apt to view success with a mistrust born of jealousy and to withhold encouragement and acceptance. Many people find it hard to be kind and natural with someone rich, famous, or smart. By withholding, or remaining somewhat aloof, they can say, "You're not any better than I am."

Intellectually, the gifted child should not march in lock step with everyone else. His mind must not be shackled. His curiosity must be protected and his growth encouraged. Some ways of doing this promote equilibrium; others do not. We should never diminish the child's gifted area in order to create a balance. Neither should we encourage growth in only one area, thereby creating a monolith.

Alexander Calder's graceful mobile makes an appropriate metaphor for a gifted child. The center of balance is the core of the child. The long wire or thread holding a large, heavy object can be seen as the child's astonishing facility in whatever form it may

10

take—math, science, art, or language, to name a few. In a mobile, the long wire or thread is balanced by two shorter wires or threads holding smaller, lighter objects. It is to these that people working with the gifted must turn their attention.

The child instinctively turns to the primary weight. It is his nature, or his calling, and he must be precisely taught in whatever field this happens to be. Unaided, he may turn exclusively in this direction, preventing balance. How much better to encourage him to find and explore the areas that will provide the secondary counterweights, bringing synergy to this mobile.

Here, the adult, parent, friend, or teacher introduces the child to knowledge or ways of thinking that he might *not* find on his own. Do parents and teachers need specific training in this technique, or do they simply need to enlarge their point of view while holding fast to common sense?

As I mentioned earlier, some adults feel intimidated or defensive with very bright children. And parents of such children are sometimes afraid to involve themselves in the child's thinking and learning, partly out of awe, and partly for fear of damaging something rare. Intellectually, this is probably a needless concern, for a vigorous mind will respond to new exposures with new growth. More important, being treated with awe by one's parents is a burden few children can tolerate. A child feels safest when his parents are kindly but firmly in charge. Without this, the boundaries all children need to test and press against are missing. Of course the boundaries and limits must expand as the child develops, but they cannot expand if they haven't been set. Remember that children need to grow socially and emotionally as well as intellectually.

Since one mark of the gifted mind is its ability to see patterns and relationships that less nimble minds might miss, the job of helping the child find secondary counterweights is less difficult or frightening than it might seem initially. The child whose genius lies in music may find fascination in mathematics or molecular structure.

11

Rhythm in sports or design may provide complementary enjoyment. Perhaps literature, pantomine, or hieroglyphics would intrigue him as a different kind of symbolic representation.

The child with a gift for history might be fascinated by geology or astronomy as a way of comprehending the enormous. Perhaps painting and sculpture as a way of knowing about people, or electronics and communications as sources of information, would provide a complement.

The whole world can be a game of attribute blocks. The gifted mind makes a lifelong search for combinations, which are endless.

Something to do, as well as something to think about, should be on the smorgasbord, whether it be cooking, painting, carving, weaving, playing an instrument, athletics, or carpentry. Gifted children have an enormous faculty for taking in information. We have to remember to give them widely varied opportunities for giving it out, too. Later chapters deal with some specific suggestions.

Caretaking, also vital, can involve smaller children, other people, community projects, plants, or a pet. Responsibility, affection, and being needed as a giver of care and nurture contribute powerfully to a positive emotional base. Caretaking forges a bond between the child and the world which the gifted child needs badly.

Because his perceptions are keen, and because he sees that he is separate from other people in his area of specialty, he needs specific opportunities to join himself to his world. Isolation is frightening to any child, and a special peril for a gifted child.

We had seen these needs, appetites, and fears firsthand and were gradually learning to understand and anticipate them.

Lucia wanted to come home after her year in boarding school to finish her secondary education at the local high school. Her experience away had not been a happy one and yet she had fulfilled her academic obligations with distinction. We were perfectly willing to follow her wish, and we and her little brother were delighted at the prospect of having her at home. The high school was a new world to her, which she entered enthusiastically. However, by midwinter the school recommended that she graduate at the end of the year. Her daily work, college board scores, National Merit placement, and the course work she had already completed indicated she had outgrown what they could offer.

There we were again in a familiar situation, one which was both complimentary and discouraging. It seemed that schools were penalizing students for outstanding work. Fortunately, Lucia remembered the lessons she had learned and wisely decided not to go to college a year early. Instead, she graduated from high school and spent a year in New York where she studied music and got a part in an off-Broadway production of *Dracula*. Blood-sucking, Beethoven, and baby-sitting were the three major ingredients of a very happy postgraduate, precollege year. Possessed by theater fever, she was admitted to the drama school of an eastern university, where she planned total immersion in theater arts. But she had a jolt one day when someone mentioned the Renaissance. She realized she didn't know whether it was a person, a place, or a thing. She saw that her education was a patchwork because of her several shifts, and decided it was time to learn some of the knowledge shared by educated people. Once again she changed institutions, this time ending up in a rigorous liberal arts program in a highly demanding college. She has just graduated with honors and is setting forth to tackle the world.

We have generalized one cardinal rule and three pleas to other families from our experiences.

The rule: Hold fast to common sense.

Three pleas:

First, try to see the gifted child primarily as a developing child. His special learning pattern is an extra, not the main thing.

Second, provide extra opportunities for emotional growth.

13

WHO THEY ARE

With a strong inner base, the child will be able to use his extra-ordinary mind even more effectively. Without it, he is just a circus performer who does breathtaking stunts, but not a whole person.

And third, introduce the child to many different kinds of thinking and doing so that he can develop the counterweights to keep his mobile balanced.

Chapter 2

Catching Quicksilver: Can We Identify the Gifted Child?

The first obstacle to identifying giftedness is a sense of embarrassment about it, both educationally and socially. The impact of such thinking on education has been either to deny that there is a group of children who are gifted, or to assume that because they are gifted they can be self-educators, use their time in school to help slower children, or do their learning outside of school where it won't have to embarrass anyone else. Apart from this philosophical problem, schools haven't wanted to single such children out because they didn't really have anything different to do with them once they had been identified.

John Silber, president of Boston University, said at the 1977 graduation exercises:

We are engaged in a headlong flight from the best.
Our flight from excellence is not a failure in our general ability to per-

15

form, nor is it the consequence of a general desire to accept the mediocre. It is something different and strange. It is profoundly philosophical: we have begun to reject the very notion of excellence as a social ideal. Out of a well-intentioned but inept concern with the equality of opportunity, we tend to reject anything if it exceeds the grasp of anyone.

Paradoxically, this rejection of excellence does not mean the end of competition. Adults and children alike still seek glory even though they may be content with laurels won from modest feats. But the wish for applause and recognition is different from the arduous pursuit of excellence. It is a mistaken assessment of quality to confuse the two, like thinking that zircons are diamonds. Denial of giftedness is a game of ostrich. Either one of these attitudes, alone, is a setback for the cause of gifted children. Together they create a gigantic obstacle.

Socially, there are equivalent problems. Some parents seek recognition vicariously through their children's achievements, and others who describe their own children as gifted are considered braggarts or liars. Competitive blood floods the cheeks of other parents required to listen to such hymning. The stage-mother, my-son-the-doctor stereotype, has fed humorists from Molière to Woody Allen.

Approaching the problem from the opposite point of view, a parent may be reluctant to have a child seem different from other children. The prodigy/freak association is automatic to some people. They may not want their child to have to take such a risk on the block, or in his sidewalk life. Henry Collis, director of the National Association for Gifted Children in London, says this reluctance is characteristic of many middle-class and lower-middle-class English families. They consider it somewhat shameful to have produced a gifted child, and often encourage the child to underachieve and conceal his ability in order to protect the family name. This is undoubtedly true, too, in some parts of the United States.

In addition to nationality, much depends on the age and cultural bias of the parents. One message of the sixties certainly was, "Away with tradition. Grow your hair. Don't dress like your parents. Be an individual. Be real." At the same time, a partner to that admonition was, "Dress just like your peers. Don't be special. Be real." Many people who grew up during those years are now of an age to be parents themselves. Some have changed their thinking, some have not.

But whatever best describes the social dilemma of the parents, woe be unto the child who proclaims himself gifted. Would even Lloyd's of London have a policy to insure his life on the playground?

A first step to improving our accuracy in identifying gifted children may be to rid ourselves of this sometimes hypocritical embarrassment and look without fear on "a society characterized by an aristocracy of achievement arising out of a democracy of opportunity."[1]

Perhaps the term *gifted* itself presents the problem. The Menuhin School in England is a school for musically gifted children, whose I.Q. scores, incidentally, range from 93 to 166. The school's admissions committee compares children to water, ice being at zero with the water getting progressively warmer. Most children might be described as poachers, or simmerers. Some might be considered boilers, but when water finally boils, part of it turns to steam. What the school unashamedly seeks are "steamers." We might all be better off if we borrowed their word since it doesn't imply its own opposite. Steamer versus nonsteamer is one thing. But gifted versus ungifted or nongifted makes an insulting distinction.

[1] George C. Robb, *Retrospects and Prospects* (London, 1975). This paper was presented at a conference held in London in 1975 and attended by delegates from fifty countries. The bibliography in the appendix includes the title of a volume of the papers presented there.

WHO THEY ARE

Whatever the reason for our embarrassment, we must overcome it and seek out reliable ways to identify the gifted children in our midst. Those who are trying to run identification programs in large school systems deserve our understanding and any help we can offer, for theirs is arduous and important work. The larger the scale, the more difficult the task, since accurate identification depends on understanding a human being, while operating a large program must depend on checklists, test scores, and figures. But complicated human beings seldom fit statistical formulae.

In a small school where teachers and students know one another well, meeting at meal time and on the playground as well as in class, the job is much easier. But the informality of a small setting does not guarantee accurate identification, and a responsible educator must be able to validate a subjective hunch. It is difficult to quantify something as mercurial as giftedness.

Let us look at some of the descriptions and criteria of giftedness, and current methods and instruments for pinpointing it, and consider their good and bad points. Then let us consider some characteristics common among people who have proven themselves gifted in hopes that this approach will help those concerned with identification to find ideas compatible with their needs.

In an effort to identify a future leadership pool and to encourage new programs, the United States Government has isolated and described the five following categories of giftedness:

1. *Intellectual.* This includes either academic achievement demonstrated by high performance or intellectual potential as indicated by an IQ score. While high intelligence surely goes hand in hand with giftedness, an IQ score can be obtained through many different kinds of instruments, some with a much greater reputation for accuracy than others. For instance, the validity of scores obtained through use of a group IQ test is poorly established, to say the least, as is the use of one final numerical score to describe an individual intellect. The reason for this is that a final number—

or full scale, to use professional terminology—is determined by combining subtotal scores from both verbal tests and performance tests. Each of these two numbers, in turn, is determined by combining the results of subtests in these two categories. The discrepancies or consistencies among these subtest scores are much more revealing than the final number, which may reflect dilution of a high score on one side by a low score on the other, or an even performance in all areas. But the final number gives no indication of its determiners. A brilliant engineer may have a very high score on the performance side and have a low verbal score. By averaging the two together it would be possible to arrive at a numerical indicator of average ability. In the same way, a well-organized and consistent student with good ability in a school setting might, through evenness of performance, score a higher number than the engineer, without any accompanying brilliance. A skillful interpreter can tell a great deal by looking at the subtest scores of a skillfully administered and scored test, but the test results are valid in direct ratio to the skill of, first, the test-giver, and then the interpreter. A well-administered test, knowledgeably interpreted, may indicate giftedness, but not certify it. I know of no test—and I doubt that there is one—that measures the strange combination, or balance, of drives and talents that produces not the numerical validation of giftedness, but rather that true miracle, a gifted person.

2. *Creative.* There are those who believe this can be measured by a standardized test. I am reluctant to join them.

3. *Leadership.* While a truly valuable gift, this, too, both transcends and escapes standardization, in my opinion. It also may be chrysalid or dormant at various times of personal development.

4. *Visual and Performing Arts.* At first glance this may seem easier to identify because there is an end product—the talents are easy to perceive and enjoy. But to distinguish between early developing of a minor talent and burgeoning genius seems a difficult distinction,

19

not predictable by timetable. A bud of something enormous does not always show as such. Similarly, a talent may grow to its ultimate capacity quickly and then stop, not heralding any further growth. The precocious child is not always gifted, nor is the gifted child always precocious.

5. *Psychomotor.* Athletes are a group that is permitted and even encouraged to excel in this country and culture. They are spotted early and given a great deal of encouragement. They are apt to have excellent coaching available either through school or municipal programs. Their teachers are quite familiar with their achievements and their parents can safely be publicly proud. Society accepts, supports, and encourages these children, and they may even get college scholarships on the basis of their muscles. Many fine athletes are also intelligent, but by no means are all good athletes intellectually inclined.

The government's method for identification leaves us with this syllogism. People who have shown themselves to be gifted are apt to have high IQs and certain character traits. Giftedness can come in the five areas listed. Therefore, anyone who is good in one of the five areas, whose IQ score falls in a given range, and who shares some of the specified character traits, is gifted.

There are two problems with using this syllogism for identifying gifted children. First, many people who have later proven to be gifted would not have been identified in school years and second, it includes too many people, exposing us to the "danger of lowering our standard of excellence through a confusion of criteria."[2]

Suppose we accept these criteria, which say that the athlete, the leader, the student, the achiever, the painter, and the musician are all gifted. Who's left?

Of course it is frequently easier to find flaws in an existing

[2]Ibid.

system than it is to design a new one. The government guidelines sprang from good intentions. They should not be rejected out of hand for their flaws any more than they should be accepted automatically because they have been published. The question we must continue to ask is whether these criteria work. Would they have identified many children we now know to be gifted?

I believe the child will keep his rightful place as the focus of our attention if we consider some traits gifted children frequently share, ways in which these traits may cluster together, and how the children use these traits in dealing with the world. I believe we will learn more by considering the effects of some of these traits, and watching *how* they are used, than we can by simply listing them in any kind of diagnostic checklist.

What follows does not pretend to be all-inclusive, but it will provide some descriptions. Those who work with gifted children (identified or not) may recognize some combinations and qualities. Some traits will seem positive, some negative. This is logical and honest because real people have both. In Chapter Four we will consider some of the delights and difficulties the gifted child faces in dealing with others in the world, but first, let's try to recognize a "steamer."

Some Traits of Gifted Minds

1. The first trait I associate with gifted minds is that *new material seems more recognized than learned.* It's as though the information, or concept, was already there and merely waiting to be quickened to life by being mentioned. This will probably be obvious in the early grades in school and may be embarrassing to the child. When algebraic equations are being explained for the first time to a class

21

of students who respond with head-scratching and knitted brows, yet one student nods with recognition and understanding, the others will surely notice. He may doodle or look out the window as camouflage.

The same kind of thing may happen to the verbally gifted child when something such as literary criticism is introduced as an art or a field of inquiry. The comment on one child's report card said, "Trying to interest Michael in sixth-grade literature is like trying to interest King Kong in a banana." It is hard for the child to handle the fact that he recognizes instantly while his peers are still struggling.

2. Another way in which a gifted mind reveals itself is in *noticing patterns:* intervals in music, shape and space in sculpture, ratio in numbers, attributes in fiction, repetitions in history. The ordinary mind can be trained to recognize these. The gifted mind does it practically automatically and delights in cross-referencing, associating the rhythm of a scherzo with the angles of a building, or the newly formed government with the shape of a constellation. Gifted children are frequently early readers, which is not surprising, since reading involves recognizing and taking meaning from patterns of visual configuration and linguistic construction.

Unconsciously and effortlessly, the gifted mind plays constantly with analogy. It is not much of a trick to solve the problem hot:cold::wet:——, but this is only the beginning. A look at the makeup of most advanced fields of inquiry shows that they require and rest on analogous thinking. This is as true of the sciences as it is of philosophy or history or art. And it certainly is true in mathematics, of which only a small part is memorization. Once the processes of computation are mastered, mathematics demands thinking, not rote memory. Intervals, comparisons, and processes come into play. Therein lies the joy and creativity. The same holds true for music (which is closely related to mathematics), architecture, literature, or science. This is why it is important to introduce the child to areas other than the one of his primary interest, so he will be aware of many possible leap-froggings.

A later chapter explores ways of finding and playing with patterns to be found in children's literature. For reasons outlined there, I believe this can be immensely comforting and rewarding to the gifted child. Patterns are around us everywhere in things we hear, see, and feel, in ways we react, and in the ways our bodies work. They are inside of us and around us in all of our environment.

3. *Energy*—this is really hard to live with! I refer to physical energy and psychological energy. Each carries impact—each is finite. Gifted children frequently need less sleep than others. No one seems to know the reason for this, but it is a trait many gifted children share. When this is understood and well managed, it needn't ruin family life. A greater than usual supply of psychological energy is the mark of many gifted people, allowing them to move at a rate greater than normal, and furthermore to continue after others have stopped. It is unrealistic and unfair to expect everyone else to keep up. Chapter Six is devoted to activities the child can pursue on his own. If the rest of the family is zonked from the trip to the museum, they can guiltlessly take off their mental shoes and relax, while the energy-generator keeps going.

4. *Curiosity* is hard to live with, too. It goes hand in hand with energy. It requires protection because it is noble and important and yet it can be annoying to a weary parent. When it annoys, it arouses a negative response. This, of course, jeopardizes it, pulling the child in two directions—wanting to get along with his parent or parents, and exercising something that insists on living.

5. *Drive and concentration.* While these are not identical qualities or manifestations, they are companions, and so I couple them. For the person who can sustain concentration for a long time it is vital to have opportunities to do so. The realities of most school situa-

tions cannot provide this, because it would be unbearable torture and unreasonable expectation for everyone else. But since we recognize what a large percentage of time is nonschool time, it will be a great relief to the child capable of long concentration to be given such chances. To be denied them, or to have the family schedule restrict them, is like wakening the child who needs eight hours of sleep a night after only four, or asking Frank Lloyd Wright to limit himself to Lincoln logs. Nascent talents and abilities must be given room and opportunity to grow or else they rankle and disturb, making for restlessness or depression.

6. *Memory*. In working with disabled children who are having trouble with memory, teachers use multisensory activities, incorporating eyes, ears, and fingers simultaneously. In this way three avenues of experience are harnessed to one specific goal and the child has a triple shot at success. As teachers, we try to join an unfamiliar fact, or concept, to one already grasped. We link the new one to something already there. Similarly, in working with children who have sparse or damaged language, we emphasize pairing, finding as many ways as possible to connect the incoming unfamiliar with the known. We work with opposites, synonyms, categories, and so forth. We teach as many ways to pair as possible. It is as though we were laying single strips of Velcro, as many as would fit, and then presenting new things as the second Velcro strip. Looking at the ways in which the disabled must work to stock their memory stores may help us understand why the gifted child remembers so much. Earlier we talked about analogy, learning, and cross-referencing of patterns, at which the gifted child is so nimble. The child who starts with an ample number of learned or recognized concepts, and is agile at connections, is like a bundle of waiting Velcro. There are so many places for incoming information to stick that, of course, it sticks firmly, in turn creating more sticking places for the next information.

Memory and memorizing are often thought of together, and

24

this brings us to a seeming paradox. While the gifted child may remember many, many things, oddly enough, he may not be known for accuracy. Strict, rote, fact memory work may not be in harmony with the quicksilver way his mind works. Memorizing the multiplication tables may have little appeal for the child who is playing with algebra in his head. While creative thinking is a higher skill than computational accuracy, the gifted child needs both to use the full range of his ability.

7. *Empathy.* The genuinely sympathetic person seems to understand others intuitively. The dictionary defines intuition as "the direct perception of truths, facts, etc., independently of any reasoning process." This is related to the kind of recognition mentioned as the first trait, but when coupled with empathy it relates to the understanding of other people's feelings, and when coupled with concepts, it relates to the cognitive as opposed to the emotional realm. Look for the person gifted in empathy as a diagnostician, a teacher, a psychiatrist, an actor, the friend to whom you take your woes, the very best hostess—all those who know how to draw others out, and who know how to comfort and heal. Since this is not a skill one can measure with a formal test, thank God, it has no numerical equivalent. It does not show on an I.Q. score, and yet is unmistakable. One can study manuals on the interpretation of body English or practice sociological diagramming, and one may strive to become a more understanding person, but although genuine empathy, based on intuitive insights, can be exercised and refined, I do not believe it can be taught.

8. *Heightened perceptions.* For the possessor, this trait is distinctly a mixed blessing (as giftedness itself may be) in that it amplifies the painful as well as the joyful, discord as well as harmony.

Gifted children usually set extremely high standards for themselves, and their heightened perceptions can throw a painfully bright light on the discrepancy between what they would like to accomplish and what they as children can in fact accomplish. This can result in a fear of failure and because failure is so painful, they may seek safety in refusing to risk.

Heightened perceptions combined with the ability to see patterns allows the child to see, intellectually, many things with which he is not ready to cope emotionally. One example is an early awareness of the discrepancy between the wished-for and the actual. Annemarie Roeper, headmistress of the Roeper City and Country Schools for Gifted Children in Bloomfield Hills, Michigan, believes this may account for the fear of death these gifted children show. This fear comes earlier to them than to their peers and seems of a greater intensity. Acceptance of the inevitability of death is a difficult emotional task for all people, but in the case of the gifted child there is a greater than normal distance between his intellectual capacity to understand and his emotional ability to accept.

His heightened perceptions allow him no room to hide from the discrepancy between his own view of himself and the world's view of him. Fusing these two images is one of the tasks of growing up for all children, but the closer the two are, the easier the task, and the farther apart they are, the more difficult the task.

9. *Invulnerability.* Current literature would say that giftedness provides invulnerability to peer pressure. There are those who believe that because the gifted child differs intellectually from his peers he has a self confidence that makes him impervious to the opinions of his peers, and immune to social pressure. Because he does not need to pursue popularity, the argument goes, he never need be a follower in order to be accepted. This is partly true.

The musical child who is composing in a new dimension will not be diverted from his explorations by the musical tastes of his contemporaries. However, in matters other than music, I believe he is just as vulnerable to peer pressure as anyone else, and perhaps more so, given his heightened perceptions and his emotional needs. Friendships are as important to the gifted child as they are to all children and friendship depends on acceptance.

10. *Divergent thinking.* As opposed to convergent thinking, this describes an enjoyment of open-ended, unanswerable questions, seeing the infinite as a treat, not a threat. While the divergent thinker is aware of what is there, he is also aware of what is missing. Think back to the example of looking at sculpture and seeing the space as well as the form or mass. In current literature on gifted children, divergent thinking is a term used as a synonym for creative thinking. It implies the power and freshness of originality.

It would be foolish to say, "Now we have a list of traits. People with these traits, or six out of the ten traits, or four out of the ten traits, are gifted and others are not." What we can say is that people who have been recognized as gifted have clusters of these traits. These work together in some mysterious alchemy to produce a gifted person. We may learn to recognize gifted children more easily than we have in the past if we think about clusters of these traits and consider the components of giftedness. We may look with more understanding eyes than before at the child who is a bother. Not all these traits are easy to live with, and the actions and thoughts they generate may rock the boat.

What group of people has been the most successful in recognizing giftedness?

Harold C. Lyon, director of education for the gifted and talented, U.S. Office of Education, reported to the World Conference on Gifted Children in London, 1975, that "We find that teachers miss 50 percent, particularly the creative youngsters, when you ask them to nominate the gifted and talented in the classrooms." Another paper presented at the same conference stated, "Parents correctly identified 76 percent of a group of Gifted Children while their teachers identified only 22 percent."

Simply the fact that these statistics, prepared by respected people and presented at a conference of leaders in the field, are so far apart illustrates the difficulty of the task. The job is complicated, as are the criteria and the children themselves.

We must not rely on the schools alone to identify gifted children, for reasons we will explore in Chapter Five. We mustn't depend on the government to do it because their categories are at once too rigid and too inclusive. They don't separate out that thin band of excellence which is found in every category from diamonds to cream, but take instead too large a number, particularly when athletes, leaders, and test-takers are all included. Orwellian perils abound. How dangerous to identify a group as the leadership elite when all late bloomers are eliminated. In order to function responsibly, we need to understand what a numerical score represents and we must be familiar with these categories, because they are part of our current language, but we must be aware of their dangers and limitations, while taking from them what is valid.

Parents and other children usually recognize something out of the ordinary. We must pay attention to what they say. As we read more, think more, observe more, we will continue to raise our own levels of awareness. As enlightened, concerned people (teachers, doctors, parents, and others), we can begin to trust our own ability to recognize giftedness when it crosses our path. We must use both objective measurements and subjective opinion. I do not believe that any single handy, reliable checklist or laboratory test is going to come along to do our recognizing for us. Human capacity is too complex for that, and for its complexity, variety, and surprises, particularly in giftedness, praise be!

Chapter 3

Hidden Talents: Disabled Gifted Children

Some gifted children come in disguise and are hard to recognize. There are those with learning disabilities, gifted children who are trapped in inhospitable socioeconomic conditions, and gifted minds imprisoned in bodies that do not serve them well.

Hidden in Learning Disabilities

Since schools put high value on verbal skills, a child who has trouble with reading, writing, or spoken expression may seem low in intelligence and therefore less valuable. And should he happen to do well in other conceptual fields such as engineering, science, or mathematics, he may be thought to be simply stubborn or lazy. "If only Charley would try as hard in English as he does in physics, he might get into a decent college."

History is filled with stories of those who did very poorly in school and subsequently made great contributions to knowledge

29

and society. Winston Churchill, Thomas Edison, William James, Woodrow Wilson, Harvey Cushing, and Albert Einstein are some well-known examples. We can learn from their stories just which language skills were difficult for them, and how these difficulties surfaced, masking the giftedness which lay beneath.

The problems Edison, Wilson, Cushing, and James shared come under the umbrella of visual association or visual memory. Edison was tutored at home by his mother for several years before he was allowed to begin school, which was not until he was eight years old. In spite of early help, he had great trouble learning the letters of the alphabet, and reading and writing were always difficult for him. Correspondence written in his late teens betrays appalling weaknesses in writing and spelling, and, although the drawings in his scientific notebooks were complicated, he appears to have limited his written words to a small number with which he had learned to be comfortable.

Woodrow Wilson did not learn the letters of the alphabet until he was nine, and he was eleven years old before he learned to read. All the while his verbal output was large and of very high quality. Harvey Cushing was plagued by spelling disorders all his life which ceased to bother him once he was free of school and could go about his business of brain surgery. Throughout his life, letters and papers were typewritten for him, and the errors he made in handwritten correspondence only served to make him seem more lovable and human. William James, avid reader and prolific writer, wrote, "I am myself a very poor visualizer, and find that I can seldom call to mind even a single letter of the alphabet in purely retinal terms. I must trace the letter by running my mental eye over its contour in order that the image of it shall have any distinctness at all."

Churchill's reputation for eloquence is surely established. Look back then at his early performance in school and see his failing grades in English, his stuttering and, perhaps underlying his

30

scholastic troubles, a difficulty in word-finding and word re-trieval. The ability to deliver the needed word at the proper time is prerequisite to ease of expression. Some people are frequently plagued by a tip-of-the-tongue aphasic feeling which hinders not only their conversation but their written expression. A bright per-son with this type of difficulty may compensate by developing a huge store of synonyms and paired associations, so that when a needed word is elusive another related word will surface to take its place. Martha frequently has trouble finding a target word but, at six, she is already quick at association. When she needed her sock last week she called it a foot-mitten. A speaker or writer who de-pends on this strategy will float from lexicon to lexicon, produc-ing originality of expression, freshness of imagery, and the sur-prise of poetry. Churchill may be one who transformed early aphasic problems into subsequent eloquence.

Einstein seems to have made his conceptual leaps directly, shortcutting the usual path of using words to formulate and refine thoughts. He was four before he spoke, did not read until he was nine, and his early school record was very poor. Later he said of himself, "The words of the language, as they are written or spo-ken, do not seem to play any role in my mechanism of thought. The psychical entities which seem to serve as elements in thought are certain signs and more or less clear images which can be volun-tarily reproduced and combined. . . . "[1] Or as Georgia O'Keeffe said in a 1977 interview for *The New York Times*, "It's as if my mind created shapes I don't know about."

Do obstacles and achievements only exist in the past?

Samy is nine years old and lives in Santa Fe, New Mexico, with his mother, who is a silversmith. His father left the United States

[1]Lloyd J. Thompson, M.D., "Language Disabilities in Men of Eminence," *The Bulletin of the Orton Society*, XIX, 1969; and Richard L. Masland, M.D., "The Advantages of Being Dyslexic," *The Bulletin of the Orton Society*, XXVI, 1976.

during the Vietnam War when he was unable to reconcile his beliefs with government requirements for military service, and has not been a part of Sam's life since babyhood. Sam's mother chose the Southwest as an area with a moderate climate, affordable for a two-person family of very limited financial resources. She has a gentle disposition and highly developed aesthetic awareness. She graduated from college with high honors in the history of art and she has accumulated an excellent collection of books. But she saves her aesthetics and refinement for her studio and shop. Home is a pigpen.

Sam had an accident when he was six months old which severely impaired the sight in his right eye. He is physically clumsy and, since his mother is a preoccupied, very permissive parent, Sam is apt to be dirty and disheveled. He makes his own breakfast, and lunch when he thinks of it. Relics of his culinary adventures decorate his clothing. Often he smells bad. He is brilliant, stubborn, and severely disabled. Three subjective statements? Hardly.

Sam gets his current events from television and has learned a great deal about history from studying the pictures in his mother's art books. And his knowledge is not compartmentalized in discrete units; he makes connections. He will talk for hours about the similarities and differences between Egyptian and Roman military equipment. He will tell you more than you could possibly care to know about various ways cities managed sewage disposal and how Leonardo's inventions resemble some very complicated ancient Egyptian and modern American machinery. He delights in connections and analogies, and has made surprisingly few incorrect assumptions. Although he has learned so much from studying pictures, and he is a nine-year-old third grader, he is just beginning to learn to read.

Sam went to kindergarten at age five. Having spent most of his life alone, or with his mother, the sight of so many other children confused and exhausted him. He didn't fit in. He was clumsy, and therefore unwelcome in the block corner. The toy kitchen held little interest for him since he had the run of a real one at home. He was very poor at scissor and crayon work, disgusted with the fruits of his own efforts, and therefore reluctant to try again. He enjoyed music, but being clumsy, bumped into other people at rhythms and could not learn to skip. The one thing he loved was the hat collection. Each one was a passport to a world of make-believe where he would gladly spend the day. His teachers worried about this and tried to coax him back to the group. Sam wouldn't be coaxed.

He went on to first grade and great failure. He could not learn his letters. They changed shape before his very eyes and represented a trap—a distraction from knowledge, not a tool for its acquisition. When his teacher tried to work with him alone he would close his eyes, put his head down on the desk, or fall off the chair. The other children isolated him. He stayed in the back of the room, silent, different, and friendless. His teacher's notes for her final report read, "Sam can't seem to learn—in a world of his own—doesn't seek out other children—flakey mother—poor eyesight—needs glasses?—retarded?"

Sam went to second grade and Kim came into his life. She was a student teacher from the learning disabilities program in a nearby college. She was scheduled to work with some small groups and was also offered the challenge of working with Sam, alone, four days a week. Resourceful, idealistic, and stubborn, she tried phonics, she tried sight words, she tried tracing, she tried primers. Sam closed his eyes, pretended to sleep, and continued to fall off his chair. But one day he gave himself away while she was reading him a story. He pretended not to care but she knew he was listening. Then a strange thing happened. If this were a fairy tale, Sam would have smiled at Kim and changed overnight into a motivated, eager, affectionate student. Sam did just the opposite. When Kim came into the room he would bump into her. During their lesson time he would yawn right in her face, and since he was unwashed, with disheveled hair and unbrushed teeth, it was very unpleasant. He seemed to be making himself as difficult and unattractive as possible to see if she would keep on trying. He learned as little from her as he could—but just enough to keep her coming back and assure him a piece of a story. Kim was discouraged. Her supervisor told her to give up on Sam, his teachers didn't think he was worth her time, yet Kim had a hunch he was bright. She saw beyond his test score and surface appearances. Sam's camouflage was doomed.

Kim read to him while he pretended not to notice, guided his hand to make him trace his letters, painstakingly taught him to recognize letters, one by one. She withheld the day's story until he had given some correct responses. Given a correct response, she would read a small bit to him, require another response, and read again. Myths and legends were his passion, and *Norse Gods and Giants* came to be their daily textbook. Letter tracing, then a paragraph about Loki, phonics cards—"L—Loki—/L/" went their lessons, then a big piece of the story with time to look at the pictures and talk. More and more, almost against his will, Sam revealed to Kim the working of his mind, the clarity of his thinking, and the depth of his knowledge. Yet he continued to start each day's lesson with some such insulting challenges as falling off the chair, spilling Kim's purse accidentally-on-purpose, or yawning in her face.

Kim requested permission to work with him again in third grade. The year had not gone far before she realized Sam had backed her into a corner. He would break his pencil point by bearing down too hard, or he would erase and tear the paper. He would listen to the story, but when the time came for letter cards, Kim realized she was leaning forward; Sam was reclining. She was active; he was passive. Her own irritation and anger finally overrode the techniques she had learned in college. She exploded, "Sam, I've had it. You're a smart kid, and you're faking. Letters are hard

34

for you, but you can do them if you stop copping out. I can't learn *for* you. No more help. No more stories till you shape up. I'm going to work with someone else." She picked up the book of myths and moved to the other side of the classroom. No response from Sam that day. No response all week. On Monday Kim and Sam pretended not to notice each other, but when she opened her purse at the end of the day she found this note:

"OK I wul red tumowor."

True to his word, Sam is struggling. He can decode three- and four-letter words now, he has memorized a hundred sight words, and can spell some of them. He and Kim are working their way through a tedious reading series for practice. Neither one pretends this is literature, but both agree it is necessary. They have an alliance against incapacity. Kim brought a high school physiology book to their lesson. She read the text, he studied the diagrams. After they had studied the chapter on preventive medicine he began to wash.

Sam loves science, biography, history, literature, and art and is discovering that he can gain access to them on his own. He is still disabled, and doubtless will always have to make a conscious effort to interpret the letters on a page, but some of his chains have been broken. His school acknowledges his intelligence. We cannot know the future, but Sam has a chance.

Hidden in Poverty

Families, schools, and community resources in economically depressed areas have special reasons for learning how poverty affects the nurture of a gifted child, how it creates distractions from recognizing giftedness, what can be done to raise levels of awareness, and what happens when unrecognized giftedness combines with lack of opportunity.

In many families where money is limited, children still receive intellectual and cultural nourishment, but the less affluent the parents, the harder it is for them to provide such costly things as tickets to plays and concerts, or music lessons. While free opportunities exist, it takes energy, time, and accurate reading to search them out, three commodities that may be scarce. Working parents may have little energy left at the end of the day for playing games, reading stories, or going on excursions.

Urban families generally live together in a small space where privacy and quiet are at a premium. There may be few opportunities for the gifted child to experiment, to be noticed, and to be recognized as gifted. When space is crowded and people are tired, families are apt to turn to television, the universal pacifier.

What about schools? Most economically depressed urban areas have old and overcrowded buildings that lack modern facilities and offer few, if any, enrichment extras. The dropout rate is high. Professional recruitment presents problems. Teachers must concentrate on discipline and physical safety before they can turn to teaching and learning. In such a climate the gifted child whose curiosity is still awake will find mischief, either in school or outside of it. The bored child with a nimble mind and restricted opportunity always finds trouble!

What about the community? Those who deal with children and social situations in economically depressed areas may not recognize giftedness because, having had little training in identifying a gifted child, they are not looking for one. Leaders of neighborhood organizations, social workers, clergy, parole officers, and guidance counselors, to name but a few, constantly deal with local problems of health, housing, crime, safety, drugs, and welfare. These usually require immediate attention. Time and energy are finite, and both have more demands on them than can be met.

Learning about gifted children may seem a low priority, or merely an academic exercise.

Yet if gifted children in these neighborhoods could be recognized and reached, they themselves could do much to help solve problems which their presence may aggravate. If their capacities for problem solving and their energies could be funneled to their own communities, the children's needs to be caretakers could be met and the problems they cause with their unchanneled restlessness would cease to exist. People concerned with social problems would find a new group of assistants replacing an old group of adversaries.

How might a community begin to raise the level of awareness of giftedness? Newspapers, radio, and television reach deeply into the neighborhoods they serve. If editorial staffs and program planners are themselves aware of giftedness and want their particular constituencies to share their awareness, it will happen. In the wake of such educational efforts, parents, community program planners, those in health, education, and welfare also become more aware. As the mesh of the sieve becomes finer, the chances of the gifted child slipping through unnoticed become fewer, and society stands to become richer.

In many ways the city and the country present different problems. But the gifted child in an economically distressed rural family may also remain unrecognized because, as is the case with his city counterpart, no one is looking for him.

Ben is one of three sons who lives with his family in a small town in the western part of New Jersey where people pride themselves on being hard-working and take satisfaction in the absence of "all them city things." The town library is in part of a house next to the post office. The school building is old, but well maintained. The town is run on a relatively small annual budget and no funds are available for educational experimentation. Most of the teachers have lived nearby all their lives, and few faculty members have had the money or inclination to continue their own studies after entering their profession.

Ben's parents own one car, which they share to get to work. His father is a maintenance man for a small manufacturing company and his mother is a hairdresser. Although there are two salaries, neither one is large; there is a mortgage to be paid on the house, and Ben's two remaining grandparents need financial assistance. On Saturdays Ben's mother takes the car to work. There is no public transportation, so Ben, his two brothers, and his father generally stay home and attend to chores around the place. On Saturday nights the family usually does the weekly marketing and then goes bowling or to a movie at the shopping mall twelve miles away, or else stays home and watches television. They get good reception on three channels and can usually see sports, situation comedies, and police shows. They cannot pick up any noncommercial educational channels. Two radio stations come in clearly. One gives continuous news, the other mingles local tidings with assorted music.

Ben's restlessness, energy, ideas, and questions are a constant irritation to his family. He is a leader in his class, but other boys' parents are beginning to mistrust him. They are afraid of what he'll think up next, and his pranks are taking an ominous turn as he grows physically stronger and his body is better able to keep up with his imagination. When he was fourteen he went on a shoplifting spree that lasted nearly all fall. He didn't need the things he took; it was the challenge of not getting caught that intrigued him. He moved from the mundane to the spectacular. He started pinching gum and Life Savers, and progressed to other things he and his friends could use such as transistor batteries and, of course, cigarette lighters. "I can get it for you wholesale," was the cry. His ultimate triumph came on a Saturday evening at the Caldor branch in the shopping mall. He swiped a pink, size 44, D cup bra. Just loitering at the ladies' underwear counter long enough to get it was a challenge. He had to keep a straight face and try not to be too noticeable—quite a trick for a gawky boy in a place where no gawky boy belonged. Once safely in the parking lot, he put it on and did bumps and grinds under the neon lights to the delight and applause of his friends. Then he threw the bra away and never stole another thing. It was too easy; the challenge was gone. He did, however, study the fine art of lockpicking. One night he walked the mile and a half to school, where he unlocked and opened every door, both inside and out—front door, science lab, record room, the principal's office, every door that had a lock. He left them all open wide, returned home, and went to sleep. The next day the school officials were horrified. Nothing had been stolen or vandalized, but they knew their safety was only thanks to the goodwill of the lockpicker. Now Ben's mind is occupied with CB radios, illegal fireworks, motorcycles, beer, and practical jokes. School bores him; team sports aren't nearly as interesting as the pranks he thinks up on his own. The dividing line between practical jokes and juvenile crime is not always clear and certainly not fair. It shifts from decade to decade, interpreter to interpreter, and social class to social class. Ben is bright and bored—a deadly combination.

A society guarantees problems for itself when it offers no appropriate channels for the energies of gifted children. As it is true in the physical sciences, it is true in human nature: energy is virtually impossible to extinguish. It can be harnessed, transformed, or stored, but not destroyed. Youthful energies—expression or suppression?

Hidden in Physical Disability

There are at least three ways in which a gifted mind can be imprisoned in a malfunctioning body. Physical immobility can stem from such neuromuscular diseases as cerebral palsy, and paralysis or distortion can be the legacy of disease or injury. Sensory impairment such as blindness or deafness can reduce the sources from which the mind takes nourishment. Debilitating chronic illness can produce peaks and valleys of physical energy whose patterns are confusing to all.

Those who are denied physical mobility, but whose capacity for intake is undisturbed, have difficulty finding sufficient stimulation or social acceptance, and they long for the companionship of kindred spirits. This combination drove Jean, the young woman we will meet in Chapters Four and Nine, to ask Virginia Gildersleeve for admission to Barnard.

While Beethoven and Milton proved through music and literature that sensory impairment need not prevent aesthetic expression, these two examples are exceptional indeed. It is a step forward for our society that today there are facilities and programs for students with sensory impairment at most universities and many graduate schools. While such programs do not guarantee success, they do promise opportunity.

A child whose giftedness is likely to remain hidden is the one who suffers from a debilitating chronic illness. Unexplained fatigue may be interpreted as laziness or poor attitude. Surprising surges of energy at odd times lead teachers and parents to say, "She's just stubborn," or "She's just not motivated," or "She can do it when she wants to." Feeling this way, they are unsympathetic when the child can't or won't, and annoyed rather than delighted by energetic accomplishments which happen at unscheduled times.

Debby had a chronic low-grade urinary infection which remained undetected until she was seventeen. From age thirteen on she complained of fatigue and minor aches and pains that seemed to have no physical origin. She asked for frequent excuses from athletics saying she got the chills outside. When she could wangle an excuse from scheduled activities, or was allowed to stay home

40

from school, she would draw. People who saw her work said, "She's just trying to get out of doing those other things so she can stay home and play with her pencil"; "A little exercise is what that girl needs to get the blood moving"; "No wonder she's pale and weak, sitting around like that all the time."

Her artistic talent was acknowledged but thought to be either seducing her away from "real life" or simply a cop-out. Her school grades were miserable. She didn't seem to bring energy, interest, or stamina to the academic fare and this made her teachers impatient and finally uninterested.

When Debby contributed ten drawings to a benefit being held for the nearby hospital, not only were they all sold, but the art critic for the newspaper praised her as an important new talent. "See what I mean," said her teacher. "When *she* wants to do something well, she can." Debby had neither the energy to meet such expectations nor the strength to fight back, so she withdrew, with the result that her drawing caused resentment rather than delight.

When she was about to enter her senior year of high school the doctor who had always given her her annual physical examination retired from practice. Debby went to a new doctor, who discovered that she had a low-grade infection. He considered Debby a legitimate patient, not a malingerer. He cured her illness and Debby bloomed. Her cheeks turned pink, her energy soared, her appetite was robust for the first time in years, and she had staying power. Her schoolwork improved dramatically without diluting her artistic output or development. People had come to assume that Debby would be wan and passive in her approach to life and had forgotten to look for the cause.

Similar stories can be told about children who suffer from such things as petit mal or chronic congestion of nose, ears, and sinuses. Of course, not all are gifted. Some are of average or below-average capacity. Not every naughty boy is gifted, nor is every child with language difficulty a Churchill or an Einstein, but it behooves us to remember Debby and Ben and Sam when we deal with children who displease and disappoint us.

Considering how many times we fail to recognize giftedness in children who are intact, it is no surprise that we frequently miss it in the disabled. We must raise our own levels of awareness and become better players in this game of hide and seek, ceasing to equate physical maneuverability and mental agility.

PART II

How They Live

Chapter 4

Give and Take

The gifted child has much to give his family, his friends, and his world. In return he needs their support and understanding. We must consider his relationships with each of these groups separately, in spite of occasional overlap, since they differ in intensity, duration, and frequency. We must also explore the special opportunities and special perils that attend each of the three; otherwise the opportunities may remain unrealized and the perils may catch the unwary by ambush.

The Gifted Child and His Family

WHAT HE CAN GIVE THEM

The gifted child will bring joy, energy, and originality to family life. These are his treasures, but they my be difficult gifts to accept or assimilate and are not guaranteed to promote domestic tranquility. When the mother of five-year-old Douglass describes

45

his early childhood, her voice blends exhaustion and awe. He was always active and seemed determined to conquer his world. His forays to the end of the crib or the far side of the wastebasket were marked by a determination Sir Edmund Hillary would have recognized instantly. In banging his mug on his highchair and pouring the milk from the mug to the floor, there was not only a delight in action and noise, but a determination to make the milk descend, and a thrill of mastery when it did. When he crept off on his first independent journey around the corner into the hall—and then urgently needed to return to his mother's side—the return trip had more a quality of reclaiming a territory than running for cover. As he investigated the new and returned to plant the flag on the previously explored, nothing was safe: cupboards, ashtrays, sisters' belongings, pocketbooks, and closets all yielded new and exciting treasures which he rearranged in novel combinations. Doesn't every woman rejoice at finding a fork in her purse? Although this child's delight in the world was contagious and, by his example, his family learned to see the novel in the familiar, it was hard to survive the combination of apartment living, ceaseless exploration, and Douglass's scant need for sleep. Infrequent short naps were all he required or would tolerate. The sharing of parental duties and allocating a generous amount of money for hiring baby-sitters saved the mother, father, and two sisters, not to mention Douglass. Now that he is five, his vigor and originality continue, but his concentration span is longer, his energies are more directed, and his scientific searches seem more like investigations than all-out invasions.

We must not confuse this child's activities, ceaseless and energetic though they were, with the restlessness of hyperactivity. His were attempts to bring the world under control, to understand it and master it. Hyperactivity is a distraction from mastery, not a step toward it.

The gifted child treats his family to a spectacle of accomplishments. These come physically as he moves out into his world using his body for exploration, intellectually as he sizes up opportunities and risks, and verbally as he learns to share his perceptions. One can say similar things about all babies. Families wait for such milestones and enjoy them with each child. But the family usually recognizes an extra dimension with the gifted child. He may walk early, as Douglass did, or, understanding the risks involved in taking off on two small feet, may wait a seemingly indecent length of time. But either his walking or his waiting will have an energetic rather than a passive quality. Words are tools of investigation and mastery, and the gifted child will probably use them at an early age, bringing delight and amusement to both speaker and listener.

The gifted child's supreme gift to his family is himself. He will share his energy and zest for exploration, and proudly parade his independence unless these have been pinched or malnourished by an unsympathetic environment. While this sounds fine on paper, it can be exhausting or maddening to live with. Lucia said, when nearly eight, "I know what I want for my birthday . . . a clothes allowance." "A clothes allowance? At your age? Whatever for?" "I don't like those boring things you make me wear. So I looked up in the Sears Roebuck catalogue and figured it out. If I just had a clothes allowance I could wear what I want." "Really? What would you buy?" The reply came solemnly, "A black dress with diamond buttons, red shoes, and a big umbrella. I could get it all for $44.37. I figured it out." Imagine the ensuing daily battle over Buster Brown oxfords with a young lady who had discovered slingbacks and rhinestones.

WHAT HIS FAMILY CAN GIVE HIM

The first thing the family of a gifted child must to do is acknowledge him as a person. This sounds obvious, but sadly, it's not automatic.

47

HOW THEY LIVE

Last spring in our school we had a call from a mother who was interested in the possibility of enrolling her child. She described him as an extraordinarily bright little boy and she wondered if we would be able to meet his academic needs. He had turned eight, was in the second grade, and she said he was bored in his present school. Admissions work is usually done in the spring, and there was nothing unusual about the call or the request. An appointment was scheduled.

It was an unusual and frightening session. The mother referred to the child variously as "my eight-year-old who does algebra in his head," "my son who is a math whiz," "my gifted child," and "the middle one who is gifted." She described his abilities, his achievements, and his test scores, but by the end of the conference, which lasted nearly an hour, she had never once used his name! We had to ask her what it was. And she clearly didn't understand the impact of our question, so totally had he become an anonymous achiever, or perhaps, her achievement.

Having acknowledged him as an individual, the gifted child's family can give him a strong connection with his world by relying on him to be a giver of care as well as a receiver. Family life provides countless opportunities for caretaking—of pets, plants, or other family members. Begun early, this tradition will be helpful throughout life. It needn't be outgrown and it needn't be shackled to the mundane. While an exotic teenage poet would probably have scant interest in taking care of a troop of Girl Scouts, she might be intrigued by the idea of growing specimen orchids or raising unusual fish. The responsibility for other living things is what forges the link.

The gifted child needs to share chores and duties as well as treats. (It goes without saying that this must be fair and not Cinderella-esque). He needs to participate in ordinary family activities as one member of the group. Joining in the telephone call to a distant grandmother, helping with the dishes, working with

48

everyone else on the Hallowe'en pumpkin, sharing the sadness that comes with loss and the anticipation of a longed-for event, talking *and listening* at the family dinner table are the kinds of group experiences the gifted child needs.

The gifted child's family can give him a reassuring acquaintance with limits and rules. This will help him structure and temper his world. Since his perceptions are acute, he sees how many things might go awry. The security of rules in his domestic life can help him tame fears of external or internal forces that might otherwise be overwhelming. Although he needs rules and requirements, he will, like all children, press at the limits, probably with extra momentum. This may intimidate individual family members, or sometimes the whole group, unless they are aware that such a possibility exists and resist the temptation to treat one child differently.

The gifted child may feel lonely because he is distinct among his contemporaries in his area of giftedness. He must not be made to feel secretive or embarrassed about his talent, and family life can provide an arena where he can display it unabashedly. This is true no matter whether the talent lies in performing, reasoning, creating, or understanding. A child loves to hear a parent say, "Will you help me? I need you." To honor a child's special quality, depend on it, don't simply praise it. Family life can give the child an opportunity to exercise it without embarrassment.

The gifted child's family must remember the depth and extent of his potential concentration and the extra power he brings to his pursuits. This combination needs scope, which his family can provide.

Sometimes the parents will need to help the child plan projects that match his level of ability and manual dexterity. This is not to say he should be held to a babyish level or have his plans thwarted. But the gifted child often has grandiose dreams; he may expect and demand perfect performance of himself and be frustrated and

49

angry when he falls short. Cooperative planning can help a child avoid this disaster. The nine-year-old boy who envisioned himself the one Saturday creator of a television set agreed to make a radio first. He had a successful experience with the intracacies of electronic diagrams and music at the end of the day. Steered away from what would have been certain disaster, this child has legitimate confidence in his ability to try the next step.

There will also be fortunate times when the child can realistically create and attempt on his own. If he is not creating his own obstacles, he should be left alone to work out his plans and projects independently.

Stimulation is important, and the gifted mind will make imaginative use of variety. The arts, nature, history, athletics (which needn't be competitive) all can reinforce one another and expand the child's receptive and expressive limits.

As interest in gifted children grows on a national scale, it is growing locally too. Many communities have Saturday programs for gifted children which offer this kind of variety, and many welcome all members of a family. The appendix includes a list of organizations and publications related to gifted children in different areas of this country. A call to a nearby group should provide current information about opportunities in a specific community. The family of a gifted child who keeps in touch with current community activities and attitudes will be able to choose those that harmonize with the family's child-raising philosophy.

The family must evaluate whatever teaching the child receives in his area of primary interest, seeing that it is precise, of the highest available quality, and demands the child's best performance. Whether the field is gymnastics, music, science, or poetry, the child must learn obedience to the discipline of his field as well as delight in its company.

While gifted children can learn from explanations and teaching, they can also hypothesize independently, as Sam the dyslexic boy in Chapter Three demonstrated. Then they need a way or place to test new hypotheses without ridicule. Such opportunities are just as important as an unending series of trips, and family life can provide them.

The child's need for privacy and enrichment are not contradictory. While he needs new experiences, new ideas, and new words as food for his intellect, he needs time, space, and privacy to play with them and internalize them. Providing the privacy in addition to the enrichment is a step some parents are embarrassed to take. Caught up in the tempo of lessons and trips, they think the child needs constant doses, and they feel guilty leaving him alone. The child's family must guarantee his privacy. He cannot do it for himself.

Living with a gifted child is not easy. It's like being invited to accompany an explorer. The reluctant or frightened parent will ignore the invitation. The cooperative parent will accept and pack for the trip. However, this is not a Sunday hike up a gentle hill. It is more like an attempt to scale the southwest face of Everest. It requires reservoirs of stamina, courage, and humor, which are the gifts the child needs to receive from his family.

SPECIAL PERILS, SPECIAL OPPORTUNITIES

It is difficult for the gifted child, his brothers and sisters, and his parents to meet their own various needs and still strike the balance most healthy families develop. For instance, it is natural for any child to try to have his own way and want to come first. The gifted child, with his extra impetus, may knock down those around him as he plays this classic game. If he always wins, he will be uneasy with himself, and the rest of the family will be resentful. A gifted child is encouraged to become a bully or a prima donna if his needs and accomplishments dominate family life. Harking back to an earlier image, three or five mobiles can swing in the same room

51

with grace and fluidity. They may be big or small, multicolored or monochromatic, depicting sailboats, paper moons, birds, orbs, or anything. As long as they are all mobiles, it doesn't matter. Set a wind-up helicopter loose in the room, and it's a different story.

It is hard for brothers or sisters of a gifted child to feel that their talents are equally appreciated unless the parents take special care. Those whose qualities are unacknowledged will naturally resent those who are favored by recognition, and jealousy will destroy family happiness. Abigail was an outstanding mathematician who loved music, literature, and any challenge to her mind. She was intellectually aggressive, yet loving and gentle in her feelings about people. Even though she was admired for her achievements, throughout her childhood she was shy and lonely. She couldn't get a tennis ball over the net until she was fourteen and, while she longed for invitations, she was bashful about extending them. She won the highest academic awards her school could bestow, and she was a National Merit scholar. But her accomplishments seemed to isolate her from other people and she often wished they were less noticed. So did her young sister, Jenny.

Jenny could walk into a room full of people, know exactly what was going on and say something to each person which showed she understood his feelings. She could make anyone laugh, and put anyone at ease, young or old, boy or girl. She found rhythm in design and athletics. She could ski, swim, and play tennis, but academics were torture to her. Jenny was jealous of Abigail's scholastic success and Abigail was puzzled and annoyed by her little sister's social ease, athletic ability, and designer touch. Since these things came easily to Jenny, she thought they were fun but not valuable. She thought things had to be difficult in order to matter. Report cards came out six times every year between September and June, and each arrival demanded a juggling act on the part of the parents. Abigail's grades must be honored and praised. It would have been wrong to give them less attention than they deserved for they were the product of unusually fine work, and intellectual accomplishment was Abigail's way of extending her hand to the world. But to interpret Jenny's miserable grades as a similar reflection of the person inside would have been to label her worthless. The report cards had to be praised and underplayed simultaneously and without hypocrisy. The parents had to encourage Abigail to trust herself, to admire her sister's strengths and try not to feel threatened by someone two years her junior who still watched *The Flintstones*. They had to encourage Jenny to trust her own judgment and ability in spite of no formal confirmation of their worth from the academic world. These two sisters learned compassion for each other and because their parents genuinely valued each child's qualities, they, in turn, learned to be proud of each other's successes. When all members of a family honor different kinds of strengths, everyone is richer. Most parents do these things instinctively unless they are talked (or shamed) out of them by those who think gifted children should be treated differently from others.

A subtle peril threatens parents of gifted children, who risk a peculiar kind of loneliness and isolation in their child-raising. The whole world is sympathetic to the family of the child on the muscular dystrophy poster. Benefits for retarded children sell out weeks in advance. Emotionally disturbed or learning-disabled children and their families can find opportunities to share their experiences and join in programs. A sympathetic ear is usually available. But try this one. Call up a friend whose child is doing creditable, average work in school and say, "I'm so worried about Johnny. He's four years ahead of his age in math and I just don't know how to handle him." Or, "The school thinks Tom ought to go to college two years early. What do you think? What should I do?" It's a quick way to lose conversational companions. Discuss labor pains, communism, your neighbor's love affair, or the recent earthquake and all is well, but introduce the dilemma of raising a gifted child and you've cleared the room. Not only must you avoid discussing the attendant problems, but you'd better not be too specific about recent successes. The threat of loneliness is as real for the parents as it is for the child.

SPECIAL OPPORTUNITIES

The world needs people who are gifted in all three dimensions of human potential: the aesthetic, the ethical, and the rational/ scientific. These labels, used by the English educator G. H. Parkyn in an address to the first World Conference on Gifted Children in London in 1975, are a memorable, simple description of a compli- cated balance. Since the happiness of the family group—perhaps even its survival—requires that the qualities of the gifted child be balanced with or against those of the other members, a unique opportunity exists here for the gifted child and his family. A group in which all three elements are represented has greater richness than one that cultivates only one or two. New ideas and thoughts can be considered in the special light that characterizes each. As the gifted child makes a particular contribution in the area which matches his talent, he covers that base, freeing the others in his family to expand in other directions. One person's talent or knowledge thus becomes not only something to be shared and admired, but also a force for new growth in other areas.

By providing opportunities for each family member to exercise all three facets of his own nature, each individual group member will have the same internal balance that is desirable for the group as a whole. The mobiles will swing without collision.

The Gifted Child and His Friends

It takes great restraint for adults not to interfere with children's choice of friends. However, except in cases of extreme unsuitability or danger, they must not usurp this privilege, although for reasons we will explore, some choices may seem puzzling.

WHAT HE CAN GIVE THEM

The gifted child brings himself, first, as the most important contribution. Since he is probably content in his own company, as most gifted children are, his offer of friendship is a step toward another person, not a flight from solitude. It is a valued gift rather than a defense against boredom.

As always, he brings energy and originality, which may not produce as many repercussions in friendship as they do in family life. Peers seem more willing to accept them, and if the going gets rough, it's possible to make new friends. Different interests may appear, new activities may have special appeal as the child grows, and the unwritten and strict code that dictates custom and costume may shift. The child is free to trade in his jeans, but not his genes.

If the gifted child seeks among his friends someone to share a particular interest, his contribution to the relationship will be depth of knowledge and the example of sustained enthusiasm. However, he may well prefer privacy in his special field, or only wish to share it with professionals.

WHAT FRIENDS CAN GIVE HIM

When adults are concerned that the gifted child's friends aren't up to his level, they must remember the frequent discrepancy between his level of intellectual functioning and his level of social maturity. A gifted child, trying so hard to measure up to his own standard of success, realistic or fantastic, can find supreme comfort in undemanding companionship. Trading baseball cards, forming clubs, sharing comic books (yes, gifted children like them, too), going to the movies, buying pizza, batting a ball, discussing disc jockeys, are all nonintellectual, normal pastimes, satisfying to a growing child. It is fun to hack around.

The gifted child needs surcease as well as stimulation. The electric, the quick, the advanced are a joy and a flint, but it is exhausting to be constantly stimulated, and nothing is sadder than the helpless creature whose gears are stuck in overdrive. Our child needs comfortable times that are not solitary. I believe this accounts for some of the puzzling alliances one sees from time to time.

Mike is a quiet boy whose electronic engineering will probably rescue the world from all its ills some day. He is in his mid-teens. When he gets home from school in the afternoon he likes to go to see Teddy, a ten-year-old neighbor. He tosses a ball with him, helps him build models, and sometimes they play with Teddy's massive collection of G. I. Joe paraphernalia which Mike passed down to him. Teddy throws himself into the make-believe and Mike finds refreshment in a bit of nostalgia. Needless to say, Teddy adores Mike, who teases him unmercifully, and both boys take nourishment from the friendship.

Susannah used to invite Maude Hart over every Saturday. Susannah's dynamism fairly rocked the planet. There was nothing she wouldn't try. Maude Hart (who was always called by both names) was a pudding of a child with tight braids, a plump face, and few ideas. Why then did Susannah beg for her week after week? Susannah was the youngest in her family. Everyone else was forceful, verbal, and independent. While she shared their talents, she stood no chance of persuading any of them to obey her. With her companion, she could call out, "Maude Hart, stand there," and Maude Hart would oblige while Susannah played out the game of the day around her, moving her from place to place as the occasion demanded, like a piece of scenery shrubbery. Maude Hart was delighted to stand in for a soldier or a lilac bush, and the two girls spent many days together—completely free from argument. Although her family would groan at the sight of Maude Hart, Susannah loved her and needed her.

A gifted child's friends may give him stimulation through a common interest. Children who share an interest, be it weather forecasting, fashion design, the Dallas Cowboys, or CB radio, contribute to one another's lives. The sharing is probably more important than the ball team chosen or the hobby itself, even though the interest may not match adult expectation.

Sometimes, of course, the interest or activity will offer rich, intellectual challenges. This is apt to be the case when a friendship jumps a generation. Warmth, leadership, knowledge, and encouragement to dare usually characterize such a relationship. Both life and literature provide examples of one older person who believes in a younger one, sharing insights and setting expectations.

A physician, renowned for his work in respiratory diseases, saw mostly adult patients in his New York City practice. Then a four-year-old boy needed his help on a regular basis for nearly two years. A tremendous bond sprang up between the two. The doctor, who was treated with awed respect by his patients and colleagues, would laugh with delight as the little boy would run past waiting room tables displaying *Forbes* and *Fortune* magazines, calling out, "Hi! I'm here. Look what I got." The child always brought his greatest treasure of the moment. The older man would examine it and then share some of his treasures in return. He gave the child a course in anatomy, showing him x-rays, explaining in detail what the pictures revealed, describing diseases and telling what kinds of medicines would help which ones. He taught the child to use a stethoscope, how to measure blood pressure, and to use long Latin names for many parts of the body. Although the little boy's illness led to some frightening episodes, and although the treatment involved both lengthy, tiring travel to the doctor's office and painful injections, the child looked forward to the visits and relished his special relationship with the older

57

man, thinking of him first as a friend, and next as a doctor. He understood and remembered his anatomy lessons and delighted in using the complicated terms the doctor taught him. If this were the script of a thirty-minute television show, the boy would win a scholarship to Harvard Medical School and the proud aged doctor would give him his own black bag in a deathbed scene, passing the mantle of healing from one generation to another. But this is a true story. After the boy's treatment was completed, the family moved halfway across the country. The boy's health remains good, and, while the young and old friend have vivid memories of one another, their current relationship is limited to Christmas cards. However, the child will never forget that a learned older person, with rooms full of mysterious shiny equipment, shared his knowledge and his time, recognizing the child's level but never stepping down to it, and instead, explaining adult mysteries in adult language.

When Virginia Gildersleeve was dean of Barnard College she arranged college admission for a young woman in her late twenties who was badly crippled from poliomyelitis, surely one of the first informal experiments in continuing education. Dean Gildersleeve believed in the young woman's ability to complete a college education and to reach her goal of going on to medical school and becoming a practicing physician. What a welcome contrast this made to other reactions of incredulity, pessimism, or ridicule. Virginia Gildersleeve had had a particularly close relationship with her own father. He had had faith in his daughter's ability to do unusual and difficult things. He had shared his ideas and thoughts with his child in much the same way the elderly physician had explained anatomy to the little boy, and he encouraged her to express her thoughts in return. Having had her own mind and dreams thus dignified in her own youth, Dean Gildersleeve knew how to do the same for others. The faith she demonstrated not only contributed warmth to the friendship between the college dean and her unusual student, but helped the young woman believe in herself at difficult times as she struggled to make her dream come true. The rest of her story is told in Chapter Nine.

The biographies of distinguished people frequently pay grateful attention to the role of an older, learned person whose friendship reached across a chronological gap to touch a younger person's mind and spirit. It may have been someone outside the family, such as the doctor and college dean mentioned here; it may have been a parent, as was the case with Virginia Gildersleeve; or it may have been a grandparent, as was the case so beautifully described in *Blackberry Winter* by Margaret Mead. Her grandmother's companionship, faith, and high expectations encouraged the young girl's explorations. Such strong, intimate relationships between people of different generations can set the direction of a whole life. In 1968 a White House task force was established for the express purpose of interviewing a group of people whose lives were particularly successful according to criteria of professional achievement and community respect to see what elements might be common to their various stories. "They all said that some individual had shed his rank and status and built an intimate one-to-one human relationship encouraging them to take risks and try new things they would not have tried without that kind of encouragement."[1]

We adults must not only notice the effect of such relationships on the children of the past but must be aware of how we may fill such spots for the children among us now.

Special Perils, Special Opportunities

Sadly, gifted children may suffer intense, unsatisfied longings for friendship, since their awareness of the ways in which they are

---

[1]Harold C. J. Lyon, *Realizing Our Potential* (London, 1975). Paper presented at World Conference on Gifted Children, London, 1975.

different makes them feel separate, since they can give an off-putting appearance of arrogance, and since frequently there is a wide gap between their social and intellectual expertise. The different child may hide in isolated eccentricity because it's safer than risking a rebuff; seeming arrogance may be a clumsy extension of a friendly hand; and a lonely child may not know how to reach out to others, and may be afraid to try. Children who need friendship the most may have the greatest difficulty in finding it. The child who feels socially unsuccessful and confuses popularity with friendship becomes vulnerable to group pressure and in exchange for acceptance, may follow the pack no matter what the direction. While this may only produce a pathetic anonymity, it may also lead to the kind of deviant, antisocial behavior we see in some gangs. The hungry child whose only social success and recognition has been tied to wrongdoing will surely continue to do wrong. It becomes his link.

The socially timid gifted child may try to conceal his special talent in an attempt to become or remain "one of the boys." Peter, the ballet dancer we will meet in Chapter Nine, tried this for a while. However, talents have a way of refusing to stay hidden. Popularity is an ephemeral prize at best, and meaningless if its price is the denial of gifts.

It is as difficult to predict the reasons for the miracle of a strong intimate friendship as it is to predict the reasons for giftedness itself, but it is wonderful to have one good friend. True friendship provides immunity from loneliness without sacrifice of self.

The Gifted Child and His World

WHAT HE CAN GIVE HIS WORLD

Once again, the gifted child offers vigorous originality. The novel ideas of gifted young thinkers may seem dangerous when they threaten traditional patterns and they may appear iconoclastic to those who cling to the status quo. Accordingly, their mental gymnastics will be accepted or rejected, depending on the point of view of the interpreter. On Charlotte's sixth-grade report card her English teacher called her original. Her sports teacher called her rebellious. Her mathematics teacher saw productive determination where her science teacher saw truculence. "Fresh" was used twice, once as a compliment and once as a reprimand. What one person called "energetic" another labeled "aggressive."

Until recently aggressiveness was suspect and unacceptable, particularly in girls. Now we seem to be growing more honest about its existence and its value. A gifted child's mental or physical explorations may seem personally aggressive when in fact they are thrustings into ideas, not thrustings against people.

Living in contemporary society is like sitting in the center of a giant corn-popper. The pot is bubbling on all sides, and things that previously looked like little brown objects with stable properties are exploding, changing shape and size, expanding and expanding. It is exciting, the results are beautiful and tasty, but the change is complete, and it is hard to say just where change will happen next. Each day seems to bring new discoveries about the human brain, past forms of life previously unknown, new theories on artificial creation of life, and all the empirical and philosophical controversy such topics generate. These few examples indicate some of the many directions thought and discovery could take.

The advent of space exploration, electronic discoveries, and technical sophistication have pushed us into a new era in which patterns of support and dependence have changed. For the first time ever tradition and culture give adults no experiential edge. Things are unfamiliar and unpredictable to all of us together. In their perception of patterns, the originality of the patterns they see, and their novel approach to traditional problems, gifted children developing into gifted adults may help us form the questions we need to ask about the future as we try to determine where our civilization should go next.

The most important thing the world can give to gifted children is a welcome and an acknowledgment of their human needs as well as of their intellectual capacities. Does this sound platitudinous? The acceptance that one group of sixth graders in a California school accorded a newcomer from New York proved to be a mirage. The group acknowledged his astonishing mathematical superiority, called attention to it, relied on it, and spoke of it proudly as a hallmark of their group. At the same time, they isolated him in this one area and turned him into their mascot. Since a mascot, by definition, is simply an object of affection, a toy or an amulet, this, of course, dehumanized him.

The child's world must acknowledge him as a human being, not as a notch in a belt or a feather in a hat. While this is a need all children share, the gifted child's own accomplishments, being outstanding, may work to his own detriment if they, alone, are the means by which his world recognizes him. If the world can accept the gifted child's extra dimension, he can accept it more easily himself. The combination of passion, energy, drive, and concentration, and his scant need for sleep are apt to exhaust most people in his world. Rather than creating delight, these traits are apt to irritate. "Why can't you——, just like everyone else?" The gifted child whose world has not accepted him is probably asking the same question of himself.

Additionally, a gifted child may be puzzled and feel faintly guilty about his extra endowment. It's the flip side of the "Why me?" we recognize in survivors and victims in other contexts. When one has less than others, "Why me?" is a natural question and is answered with sympathy by society. When one has more than others, "Why me?" is frequently answered with some version of "Why you indeed?" Scant comfort. In accepting the child, the world admits his qualities and removes his need to feel guilty, giving him license to use his energy for growth rather than for expiation or disguise.

The world can give the gifted child a mirror off which to bounce his various reflections so he may choose which ones are accurate and which ones are only temporarily satisfying dramatic exercises. As a little child, Claire was by turns the intrepid explorer, the detective, the monster, and, in later years, the egghead, the dilettante, and the embodiment of ennui. At seventeen she was in real danger because she had not held back one corner of her mind for realistic appraisal. She couldn't tell which pose was real and which a masquerade. The gifted child who finds welcome, acceptance, and reflection in the world around him will be able to resist the Circean call to eccentricity. While it may seem fun to play Greta Garbo or Oscar Wilde temporarily, it is frightening to be marooned in make-believe.

The gifted child's world can provide opportunity and exposure. This needn't mean extensive travel through the Himalayas; it can happen in neighborhoods, cities, villages, or country towns. It's a question of the point of view. If financial strictures preclude travel, libraries have books and records, children have feet and one another, and television broadcasts some excellent materials. Neighborhood excursions can yield a wealth of information and provoke profound questions. There is a sunset every day, but we frequently run out of time to notice it.

SPECIAL PERILS, SPECIAL OPPORTUNITIES

The gifted child is in danger of feeling like Superman, invulnerable and invincible. One four-year-old child, who frequently sees frontier where his family sees only peril, set off on an independent foray into the world, absorbed in his exploration, confident of his destination, and unperturbed at the prospect of a return trip. He lives close to a dangerously busy highway and to a swamp. When they realized he was missing, his family scoured the house and the neighborhood. He had been scolded severely several times in the recent past for running away, and they couldn't believe he had done it again. They were sure some dreadful trap had caught him. They finally found him several miles away, standing in a clump of trees. At first they were filled with joy at seeing him safe and alive and said, "We're so relieved to find you. What are you doing here?" He said, "I wanted to see the owl. I have one in my book." Indeed, his father remembered that six or eight months ago he had spotted an owl in this very tree and had shown it to the little boy. Relief turned to anger. "But you know you're not allowed to run away. We've told you and told you." "But I wasn't running *away*," protested the child, "I was coming to see the owl." He didn't understand their concern any more than they understood his insouciance.

An athletically gifted child may come to feel invincible. This feeling encourages prowess and prowess is nourishing. With it, a child sees himself not as a leaf carried on the stream, but rather as a determining oar in the water. All to the good. The danger here is that physical prowess is so often displayed in a competitive arena. The child becomes accustomed to a cycle of win-develop-compete-win and, being gifted, wins many times. Winning then becomes part of his identity, in his own mind, as well as in that of eager coach, proud parents, and admiring onlookers. Thus, when the inevitable moment comes to lose, it is as though a genuine part of his identity is lost. It is not an event; it is an amputation.

Intellectually, a subtle peril exists for the gifted child who is trying to explain new insights. Original ideas are difficult to express and even great thinkers may have trouble developing new symbols. Using old symbols in new ways is confusing to those of us who are trying to interpret by habit. We are used to certain symbols and patterns and don't stop to think about them every time we see or hear them. When the thinker or artist comes along who uses the familiar in unfamiliar ways, we are apt to react with suspicion or discomfort. e. e. cummings was initially considered crazy and dangerous, as were Stravinsky and Frank Lloyd Wright. Very few major contributors to science, philosophy, or the arts found acceptance early in their careers.

Finally, unless concerned adults are alert, gifted children are in danger of being exploited. They are being discovered as a new profitable commercial market and the "maximizers" and the "utilizers" smell gold.

For good or ill, we are a nation of bandwagoners with a cultural reflex demanding that once a condition is labeled, society must develop methods for either succumbing to it or curing it. From clean laundry to bad breath, we mobilize. Giftedness is no exception. Many of the materials being developed for gifted children to use at home, in school, or as independent projects are delightful and instructive. We and the children in our care should welcome them and learn how best to use them. But we also face an avalanche of "identificational instruments" and kits purportedly designed to foster creativity but which, in reality, are packaged and sold by humorless pedants.

In one three-week period my professional and personal mail included advertisements for over twenty-five items labeled specifically for gifted children. They ranged from materials for a set of classroom science experiments, which appeared to be of very high quality, to *Crossword Puzzles for Gifted Children, Grade 2*. The latter was actually a repackaging of a softcover book of the same crossword puzzles previously labeled for grade four. Another brochure assured me that if, as a teacher, I needed to spend funds allocated for materials for gifted children, or G/Ts as they were called, I could order the new lit kit containing condensed paperback versions of the classics complete with comprehension questions. They further assured me that "flowchart-wise," over 50 percent of their offerings were materials for G/Ts.

There is nothing intrinsically evil about giving fourth-grade crossword puzzles to a second grader, and abridged versions of complicated stories can be appropriate, but surely truth in labeling is as important here as it is in the supermarket. We should know what ingredients are in the nourishment we buy for children's minds as well as what goes into the food we buy for their bodies.

Will it be long before we have such terms as "Gift-speak" to describe the utterances of gifted children, followed by "Insta-Gift-Speak," a kit to help a child be among the first to qualify for a new program? As British society was humorously divided into "U" and "non-U," will we be "G" and "non-G"?

Gifted children need protection from such exploitation. The power and freshness of their genuinely creative thinking must be protected, and their humor and creativity must be insulated from those materials that cap creativity while claiming to unlock it. They need people who insist on seeing them as real live people, not "ideational models" or percentages of populations.

Whether learning-disabled, retarded, handicapped, or gifted, it is inevitable that once a special category of student is identified, people have to be found to fit the description. School districts have money to be spent on their behalf, teachers have been specially trained and hired to cope with them, and educational materials have been developed and must be bought. With all this ready and waiting, each district needs to produce some such students in order to keep up with neighboring districts and keep the grant money flowing. Think what would happen to land values if the Elmwood District said, "We have only three gifted children this year. We don't need that program," while Oakwood was saying, "Gifted children make up 33 percent of our student body. We need more facilities." Families would surge to Oakwood, hoping there was some miraculous mineral in the drinking water.

It is heartening that gifted children and their needs are being given their rightful turn in the spotlight and that many adults are working wisely and enthusiastically on their behalf. But it would be destructively naive to assume altruism and quality in all the programs and materials which today claim to be for the gifted.

While it is not simple to live with a gifted child, humor and resilience can make the way easier for all concerned. Those who learn to understand and accept the drives these children have can share an adventure. To return to our earlier image of accompanying an explorer, new sights and experiences will be ours if we will go with him to a land we could not find on our own.

Chapter 5

A Goodness of Fit: The Gifted Child and School

Just as a choral director would be sure to hand a soprano score to a soprano, and an Olympic aspirant would only train with equipment appropriate to his physical size and level of skill, the gifted child will blossom best in a school which provides "a goodness of fit." This phrase, attributed to the late Herbert Birch, New York physician and professor, describes an ideal match of student need and academic offering. In stressing the harmony of the combination rather than the merit of a particular program or child, this concept underscores the flexibility and understanding gifted children require.

No single institution, family, or school can be expected to meet all of the needs of any child. The school certainly cannot do it alone. But the family, the school, and the student himself (in a manner appropriate to his age) can cooperate in meshing available opportunities and the student's academic, social, and emotional requirements to create a "goodness of fit." A brief review of recent educational changes may help us understand what the school can and cannot promise the gifted child.

In times past, parents expected schools to concentrate on the child's intellectual training, but now schools are expected to provide for the whole child. More and more, parents depend on schools to function in loco parentis, taking responsibility for the child's social and athletic life as well as his intellectual and moral growth, psychological well-being, and his plans for the future. The guidance office is frequently busier than the library.

Changes have come in facilities as well as in functions, giving us many different kinds of schools. The rapid growth of the suburbs and the popularity of large families in the fifties and sixties spawned new schools in existing communities and new schools in new communities. At this moment in this nation we have public schools, parochial schools, and independent schools, all operating at elementary, junior high, and high school levels. They are urban, rural, well supported, well equipped, poorly supported, poorly equipped, with every variety of size, student body, and faculty. Some are close to colleges that offer teacher-training programs and hence have a steady flow of student teachers or apprentices. Some are well equipped with libraries, stages, music and art rooms, gymnasiums, darkrooms, and sometimes computers. Some schools are isolated, others are centrally located but lack facilities. Because of such great variety, and the variety of the children themselves, it would be foolish to try to devise an ideal curriculum for a gifted child here. But we can consider ways to tailor a goodness of fit between the gifted child and whatever school he may attend, whether the combination is ideal, workable, or miserable.

It is ideal when the school and the child are together by choice. A family may hope to choose a particular public school by buying or renting in one residential area. When this works out, all is well, but recent history shows that because of busing, or redistricting, or taxpayer revolts, there is no guarantee of permanence.

70

Some families prefer independent schools. Students come by choice and the school is free to accept or reject an application. Of course this does not guarantee perpetual peace but it makes a healthy beginning, and since there is mutual freedom to change, no one is in a trap. Each year the contract is renewed if both sides so wish.

In some instances there is no choice at all.

The wise family will try to work in harmony with whatever school the child attends. They will acknowledge what the school does well and voice their appreciation. Thoughtful educators will respond in kind. Once a cooperative climate has been established, school, family, and student can decide which areas of the child's life may need more attention or different levels of activity and parcel out the responsibility. The child himself should have an active stake in his own learning and not simply be the passive recipient of planning and attention.

Traditionally, the child's academic needs are met in school with the family lending support at home. Social needs are taken care of by both school and family. The responsibility for meeting emotional needs rests primarily with the family, whose efforts are supported by teachers in the school. In spite of good intentions on all sides, however, the boundaries sometimes shift. The following stories of five children show different ways this can happen.

Michael was in the sixth grade in an independent boys' school in the Midwest. It was strong in traditional academics, and offered an outstanding athletic program. Discipline was firm, studies were carefully sequenced, and grades were given and posted regularly. Michael was an able student and an excellent athlete. The school met his needs well in these two areas, but Michael was also a gifted pianist, and had a gentle, loving side to his nature. After much deliberation, the school agreed to allow Michael to substitute piano (lessons and practice) for one of the regularly scheduled daily study halls. In addition, his family enrolled Michael in a

71

Saturday program at their community nature center where he not only learned about animals and plants but shared in their maintenance and care. All the children in the program were given opportunities to take both plants and animals home during the week, loving them and tending them, to be sure, but also keeping scientific records. No grandparent has ever been prouder of offspring than Michael was of the hamsters born at his house. The mother hamster's chart was a careful record of gestation period, diet, onset and length of labor, time of delivery, and observations of the general health of mother and babies. Cooperative planning by Michael's teachers and family created a goodness of fit between the child and his education. He loved his school day, particularly after piano instruction became a part of it, and both his affective needs and his needs for independent study were satisfied by the nature center program.

Martha was in the fourth grade in an open classroom, public elementary school in the outskirts of a northeastern city. The atmosphere was permissive and the arts were heavily emphasized. The curriculum was individualized and students seemed to use the discovery method for everything from the principles of gravity to the multiplication tables. Martha was high-strung, artistic, and independent, and happy in a school that catered individually to her rapid pace and creative spurts. However, the school and her family wisely decided that Martha needed some firm, recognizable structure, too. So she joined a children's choir, which provided a very disciplined artistic group activity, and she began what is now a valuable coin collection. She loved the beauty of some of the coins and also learned to appreciate their history, how they were made, and their relative value. She created highly appealing methods of display and thoroughly enjoyed acquiring large amounts of precise information.

Jeffrey's school urged him to join a Saturday club for gifted children on a university campus two hours away from his home. Fascinated by computers, he had learned all that the teachers in his own school could teach him. He was capable of astounding feats and needed the kind of advanced facilities available only at the university. It seemed a miracle that an appropriate program existed. Jeffrey's parents were unsophisticated and afraid to be different. They were frightened by the school's suggestion, interpreting it as a version of expulsion. They were afraid of the people Jeffrey might meet, and what their neighbors would say. They wondered how to explain that Jeffrey wouldn't be around for local Saturday events such as bowling and Little League. They wondered if people would think they were trying to show off. They worried about the expense. But they agreed to give it a try. The experiment was a total success! Jeffrey continued to enjoy his classmates, got in an appropriate number of disciplinary scrapes for playing rowdy games of floor hockey in the corridor, and received his greatest intellectual nourishment away from school with other people who understood his thoughts.

The foregoing are all happy stories. Unfortunately, conflict and antagonism sometimes prevent cooperation.

When the choice does not exist, a family may try to change the character of a school. Such efforts seldom help the child since educators rarely welcome parental interference with curriculum.

Where controversy seems imminent, the child's best interests are served by a thoughtful family who is more interested in the child's well-being than in having the last word. Realistically, the family is the child's primary resource, and it is easier for a family to modify its schedule or change the activities it emphasizes than it is for a school to do so.

In situations where a goodness of fit is difficult or impossible to arrange, it may help the family to remember that although school is a legal requirement, and therefore an inescapable reality for the child and his family, and although it absorbs the central block of the child's time on Mondays through Fridays, it doesn't take it all.

HOW THEY LIVE

There are the years before school, and the hours and days when school is not in session. For example, in New York State, schools are required to be in session 181 days, six hours per day. That leaves eighteen other hours in every day and even adolescents seldom sleep more than ten of those. There are 184 days, virtually half the calendar year, when there is no school at all.

This realization made life bearable for Eric, who hates school. He is in seventh grade in public school in a medium-sized town in Mississippi. His mother is an operating room nurse at the local hospital. His father has a debilitating heart condition and cannot work. Eric is a mathematician and a contemplator, small for his age, and not particularly athletic. He would be very comfortable with college mathematics, but those in charge of his school program rigidly insist on his taking the same math courses as his classmates, and no others. They say it is good for him to be treated the same as everybody else. They point out that he is not particularly well liked by the other students and does not do well in athletics. "He'd better learn to make a place for himself, just like everybody else. No special favors." They feel that the example of an inactive father has encouraged the boy to be different—"too much thinking—an oddball." They resent his mother's efforts to change his curriculum and mistrust her for the clarity of her thinking, her knowledge, and the ease with which she expresses herself. She is a threat and they are jealously guarding their prerogatives. Eric is trapped. He is required by law to attend this school. He cannot physically leave it. He needs to remember that he has time before and after school to do as he wishes; to think, explore, experiment, and read. He continues to play games of strategy with his father and they have joined a club to play chess by mail. He got a dog for his birthday. During school hours, Eric has to insure his intellectual privacy by handing in his assignments promptly and by being unobtrusive. His junior high school sentence has nearly been served.

74

Paul's school was also reluctant to promote his intellectual growth but for different reasons. His parents wanted to enroll him in first grade in a nearby independent school. He was nearly five, could read well, and had good number concepts. However, since the head of the lower school felt he was chronologically young and socially extremely immature, she offered him a place in kindergarten instead. For the first three months of school, Paul was a bystander. After Thanksgiving he began to try to join in activities in the block corner and made small experiments with messy paint and conversation. By February he had a friend. Unsatisfied, his family wanted him to have more workbooks. Both his teacher and the head of the lower school gave examples of how Paul was growing as a person but the family did not share their enthusiasm or understand their priorities. Without telling them, Paul's parents hired a private tutor to work with him every afternoon in reading and arithmetic. Paul began to suck his thumb in school, and went back to the sidelines. The school voiced concern over his regression, but the parents remained silent about the afternoon lessons. In May Paul's mother called to say he would not be returning the following year. They had found a school willing to put him in the third grade. It seems unlikely that Paul will be given the chances for emotional and social growth he needs so badly and to which he was beginning to respond.

Identification of Gifted Children in School

Schools that offer special programs for gifted children generally rely on two measures for identification: marks and money.

High academic achievement is the most commonly used yardstick even though it alone does not certify giftedness.

When good marks are the result of a fine mind growing in an academically challenging situation, hymns of Thanksgiving

75

should fill the air, and student and school should be left in peace. But if the school lacks academic rigor, the same grades don't mean the same thing. Furthermore, it is always vital to consider how much of the student's personal energy is directed to report card success. If high grades are one of several elements in a child's life, they indicate balance. If high grades are the major goal of the child's life, they indicate distortion. The Grind is both caricature and cliché. A student who is socially timid may find schoolwork a safe and polite way of hiding from people. In such a case, he invites impoverishment rather than enrichment from his academic labors.

As good marks do not always indicate giftedness, so mediocre or low grades do not always indicate dullness. If the work is too easy, or requires conformity instead of thought, the gifted child may be bored and may not score well. If he is interested in the social doings of his classmates and is not being intellectually stimulated, his energies will flow in social directions. If he is at odds with his teacher, he may be unwilling to apply himself. If he is afraid of not satisfying his own expectations, he may refuse to try as a way of avoiding failure. Each of those attitudes will result in poor grades which are not caused by poor intellectual endowment. We considered the disabled gifted child in Chapter Three, but it is important to mention again that schools value verbal skills. A child with modest verbal skills may be highly gifted in other areas that are not reflected in marks. Unless we understand the reasons behind high or low academic performance we cannot interpret the goodness of fit between the child's ability and his report card.

All too often, when a school system decides to offer a special program for gifted children, the number of available dollars determines the makeup of the group. A school with a generous allocation of funds will probably identify many. A school with limited funds may not dare to identify more than a few. This is not necessarily an accurate way to select or reject a child as gifted. In one

Westchester County town gifted children were an unknown until $2,500 became available for an elementary level program. Then followed a well-publicized school board dispute. One faction spoke against the entire program because they did not feel the preparation was sufficiently detailed. The winning faction felt that since the money was available, there was no risk in going ahead. Students for that program were to be selected on the basis of IQ scores obtained from a group administered test and standardized test scores. Finally, "the program itself shall determine the number of pupils selected for inclusion." What effect will this have on the children? Are those chosen by this method in fact the gifted children in the school? Will they cease to be gifted next year if the cash flow dries up and become de-gifted or dys-gifted? Budgets are a reality of life, and doubtless the planners of this program are well-intentioned, but the episode illustrates one reason why schools are not always accurate in identifying their gifted students and why we must not rely solely on them to make such decisions.

What is likely to be the impact on the rest of the school when one group is identified as gifted? Usually there is a different reaction in each group within the school: faculty and administration, other students, and parents.

The size of the budget will influence or determine the reaction of faculty and administration. If the budget is ample and facilities and extra personnel are available, the faculty may well react with joy and pride. Intellectual vigor is contagious and a teacher who is part of an academically outstanding institution can enjoy the stimulation. However, if a group of special children is identified and there is inadequate funding, the teachers and administrators may be far from jubilant. Resistance will generate such comments as "Mainstreaming is the ideal," "This is supposed to be a democracy, isn't it?" "The bright ones can do it on their own." The addition of one more special program or individualized curriculum may seem overwhelming if present class size and demands on time have already led to faculty fatigue.

Other students will probably accept the identification of a special group more easily than either teachers or parents. Children know when another child has an extra dimension, and are usually forthright about acknowledging it. If children are assured that their own contributions are valuable, they will not resent others being singled out for something different. If artistic talent, athletic ability, academic achievement, and citizenship are all recognized, each student can feel enriched, not diminished, by another's special gifts.

Parents react vigorously when a school labels one group of students as gifted. Those whose children are chosen show their pride according to their personalities; they may preen, boast, glow quietly, or be embarrassed. Parents whose children are not chosen usually react as people do when they are excluded, again depending on their personalities. They may object to the concept of identification, to the instruments used, to the children chosen, or to the teachers who were responsible for the selection. But whatever they specifically object to, or whatever form the objection takes, the chances are that they will be hurt or angry. The danger is that they may take out their disappointment on their own child or children, pressuring them to try harder to get on the list. Adult reactions of jealousy, resentment, or denial will spill over onto the children and bring about a childhood mirroring of adult negatives.

Ideally, a parent-education program precedes a program of identification. When schools make the effort to help interested parents understand the problems as well as the blessings of giftedness, much potential jealousy will disappear. When parents understand why a program is necessary for gifted children they are likely to respect it, support it, and may even volunteer to serve in it. Teachers are a necessary part of such a parent-education program, and as they share their professional knowledge with nonprofessional parents they too will raise their own levels of understanding of giftedness, and recognize what the school can and cannot give each gifted child.

The Teacher

The success of the program depends on the teacher.

This cannot be said too often or too loudly. The teacher's personal style and point of view are more important than the number of courses taken or certificates received. In addition to being knowledgeable about subject matter, the teacher must enjoy meeting special needs, admire independent thinking, and welcome challenge.

Most teachers have homerooms or teach special disciplines such as mathematics, history, a foreign language, science, or English. They must juggle the needs of regular students and those of children with special requirements. Oddly, the presence of gifted children in regular classes will arouse the same set of responses as the presence of disabled children. Both represent special needs. Some teachers will be exhilarated, and their creativity will be stimulated. Others will try hard and their success will be in direct ratio to their flexibility and imagination. Others who feel threatened by giftedness will resent the child.

We know that the divergent thinking described in Chapter Two is a common trait of gifted minds. The student whose responses to straightforward questions spring from divergent thoughts is a delight to the teacher who admires independence but is an unwelcome challenge to a teacher who likes to dispense knowledge and hear it parroted. Oblique answers and unusual ideas are threatening to a teacher whose goal is to control. There will probably be no goodness of fit between such a teacher and a gifted child.

Power and excitement will characterize the relationship between a gifted child and a supportive teacher. Encouragement can lead a child to love a subject he might never have thought appealing. This can happen in the classroom or outside of it. Adult willingness to share an enthusiasm is contagious. If enthusiasm is coupled with both knowledge and experience, the child can learn from the adult. If the adult has enthusiasm, and incomplete knowledge, the older and the younger can explore together. No adult is ever made smaller in a child's eyes by saying, "I don't know." The child is honored when the adult says, "I don't know, let's try to find out together."

Three Approaches

There are three philosophical approaches to the education of gifted children: acceleration, segregation, and enrichment.

ACCELERATION

This was a frequent choice in the past. It seemed easy and convenient since it was available and didn't require extra money. But as more people understand the social and emotional perils involved, the disadvantages are being recognized.

It is very difficult for a child to be separated from his chronological peers, even though his intellectual capacity in certain fields may extend well beyond their grasp. We know that children pass through certain developmental stages on their way to autonomy. Children in an accelerated program who try to skip over some of these stages miss the accompanying activities. Lucia leapfrogged over the era of the secret club, missing the fun of the membership list, election of officers, selection of the password, location of meetings, and then the agony of trying to think up a suitable secret. There is a year in school when such clubs flourish. Children

80

who are one year older have outgrown them, and children one year younger don't know how to put them together. How sad it was for her to be too young to be included when it was de rigueur, and alone in needing it when others had outgrown it! In rushing to close a permanent chronological gap, the child who tags after others' pleasures misses his own.

An intellectually gifted sixth-grade reader still needs to read sixth-grade stories with other sixth-graders to share a common emotional reaction. His reading needn't be restricted to this, but must include it.

The child who is conceptually brilliant in mathematics or science needs to be with his age group at least part of the time for this reason. Unless the child is included in classroom explanations, he may accumulate his mechanical skills in a haphazard way. Since he appears to know so much at an advanced level, people may incorrectly assume that he has understood each earlier level. Brilliant minds need accuracy and discipline. The ability to see new patterns or to extend an idea beyond the reach of ordinary minds is dazzling, and anyone with the smallest element of P. T. Barnum in him is surely going to be tempted to pyrotechnics. Without precision and an understanding of hierarchical process the child's performance can be impressive, but superficial cleverness may keep him from profound understanding. Real skill depends on discipline.

From the opposite point of view, technical accuracy without brilliance produces the reliable but not the profound. The gifted child needs the accurate mechanical skills of his field as well as the original thoughts in order to develop his talent to its utmost capacity. Using both meanings of the word prevent (impede and precede) we can say that facileness prevents profundity.

The social and emotional drawbacks to acceleration outweigh the advantages of arriving at the end of formal schooling one or two years ahead of schedule.

81

HOW THEY LIVE

Segregation means separate programs. We should consider examples of those that physically remove students from their regular school, those that exist within the regular school, those devoted to one particular academic discipline, and finally, those that exist because of the special nature of the school itself.

One public school program in a northeastern city provides that students in the district who qualify as gifted shall attend their regular school three days a week and be transported to a special center two days a week. There they work on projects deemed to be stimulating. Those in charge of the program assume that because the children are clever they will catch up on Monday with whatever happened in their absence on Thursday and Friday. This program is only two years old and may ultimately prove successful. However, so far it has aroused tremendous uneasiness and resentment in the community. Parents are competing ferociously to have their children included. Local psychometricians can scarcely keep up with the demand for testing. Monday through Wednesday teachers are resentful. "I'm good enough to teach him and watch over him in the beginning of the week but I don't qualify on Thursday and Friday." "What am I supposed to do?" "He'll get all that extra stuff over there in that special place, I don't need to do anything different for him." Teachers who are trying to organize a dramatic program or build a varsity team find half their people missing, and the students, both the selected and the leftovers, are thoroughly confused.

Some segregation programs take place within the regular framework. Schools, either public or independent, which group students by ability automatically offer this in their honors sections or tracks, whichever term they choose to use. In secondary school this works well. Students remain with their contemporaries, and can still eat lunch or play basketball with friends who may not be

82

in their calculus class. Teachers enjoy teaching advanced sections. There is seldom a discipline problem, and the students are usually receptive and quick to understand. However, for elementary school years, this kind of segregation is usually not appropriate.

Some segregation programs exist for a special purpose, such as the SMPY (Study of Mathematically Precocious Youth) at Johns Hopkins University in Baltimore. This program attempts to identify seventh-grade children with extraordinary mathematical abilities and then to act as a catalyst. Although some direct teaching is involved, the main goal is to spot these children and help them accelerate their studies. Frequently a child is encouraged to go straight to college, without reference to his chronological age. A recent example is Eric Jablow, who joined the study at age eleven and now, a college graduate at fifteen, has entered Princeton where he hopes to earn a doctorate in mathematics. Although SMPY is philosophically comfortable with the kind of acceleration which isolates a child from others of his chronological age and which fosters growth in only one area, they also promote some extracurricular after-school, weekend, and summer programs.

Finally there are segregation programs that are defined by the very nature of the schools.

Hunter College Campus Schools in New York City is an example. Founded roughly one hundred years ago, and operating under the aegis of the New York City Board of Higher Education, this school has 1200 high school students whose IQs, as measured by the Stanford-Binet, are frequently 155 or 160. Students in this school are with their chronological and intellectual peers every day. This is an exciting and rare opportunity. However, according to Dr. Bernard Miller, director of the school, there are not nearly enough openings to satisfy the number of applicants. "It's a wonderful school but it's practically impossible to go here."

Since independent schools are free to choose their student body and curriculum without state control, they can tailor programs to

83

specific groups or needs, depending on student body, faculty, and community expectation, and can readjust to achieve goodness of fit.

Roeper City and Country School is a coeducational school for gifted and talented students in Bloomfield Hills, Michigan, with an enrollment of 500 students, 307 in the elementary division and 193 in grades seven through twelve. By nature and title this school exists for a distinct population. It goes without saying that their academic standards are high, and it is interesting to note that in their admissions policy and their curriculum they do not look for a single score or a single focus, but stress instead combinations of talents, observation and manipulation of patterns, and the development of the child as a human being.

Independent day schools can offer segregation to gifted children, as Roeper does, if that is what the community requests and is willing to support. Or they can represent an alternative to public education which, by philosophy and teaching methods, can accommodate gifted students and other students too.

Marcus was miserable in his local public school near Philadelphia. As early as second grade his giftedness in mathematics was unmistakable. When he reached third grade his school was either unable or unwilling to offer him the kind of teaching he needed. He grew frustrated and bored. His family had always believed in public education and felt that independent schools were somehow un-American. However, their child's unhappiness forced them to investigate some of the nearby alternatives. Feeling traitorous to their own ideals, they switched him in midyear to a country day school. He joined a class of eighteen children, one of whom had severe learning disabilities, three of whom needed extensive remedial reading, and the rest of whom were solid or outstanding scholars. Following the lead of a strong teacher, the children enjoyed one another, and while recognizing their various differences, neither mocked those in difficulty nor salaamed the very able. They willingly made room for Marcus in the group. A spe-

84

cial mathematics curriculum was designed for him, and he did his other work with the rest of his class. His family was thrilled with the democratic spirit reflected in the balance and activities of the whole class, and overcame their initial feeling that independent education was equivalent to social snobbery.

Many nationally known secondary schools offer segregation of the gifted by the very nature of their student body. A child must be very able in order to be admitted to such schools as Exeter, Andover, and those special purpose public high schools that still exist. Many incoming students each year will have scored in the ninety-ninth percentile in the Secondary School Aptitude Tests (SSAT). Segregation is doubled in a boarding school which requires living twenty-four hours a day with intellectual and chronological peers. Here lies the value of the school's freedom to select its student body. A wise school will orchestrate a good balance of rational/scientific, aesthetic, and ethical/moral strengths in the student body as well as the faculty. The gifted boy or girl who goes to such a school should find a combination of intellectual challenge and opportunities for healthy social and emotional development.

ENRICHMENT

Enrichment can be provided in three ways. Independent projects can be available during school hours as part of a child's curriculum. Wise planners realize that enrichment doesn't mean more math dittos, but fewer, once the child has demonstrated understanding of a concept. Extracurricular activities can also be a regularly scheduled part of the academic day and there can be afterschool, Saturday, or weekend projects. These three approaches are not mutually exclusive, they do not conflict with one another or with the regular curriculum, and they need not be expensive.

In elementary school, where children work in a self-contained classroom, an imaginative teacher can provide enrichment as a part of the curriculum. Something such as a special project on dinosaurs could be available to those whose work is completed, or perhaps a unit on Morse and semaphore code could replace some regular assignments. There is no limit to suitable ideas. (Some of the suggestions in Chapter Seven on group activities may be helpful.) It is as easy to supply enrichment in a traditionally arranged elementary classroom as it is in an open classroom. The teacher's priorities are more important determiners than the arrangements of the tables and chairs.

Enrichment can still be part of the regular school day in middle grades when children generally have a homeroom and go out to different rooms and teachers for separate subjects. The homeroom teacher can provide brain-teasers for children to work on alone, in pairs or in small groups. Some of these can doubtless be incorporated into particular subject matter. A teacher can stock some of the excellent commercially developed games of logic, vocabulary, or pattern, and a creative teacher will develop many original ones. Middle school teachers who do not have homeroom groups can do the same thing. This is not to suggest that a Scrabble game in every bookcase will take care of the gifted children from September through June. Of course more is needed. But it is important to remember that enrichment can take place in many hours of school and home life. It needn't be limited to a special period of the day. Children's lives needn't resemble television programming with special slots for housewife time, the children's hour, and family viewing. The whole day can be prime time.

When they reach high school, students have more freedom to choose their courses. Independent study projects can be arranged more easily than in earlier years. Since students are more likely to carry out such projects successfully, administrators are more likely to endorse them. In addition, honors sections are frequently available and no stigma is attached to membership. The student whose enthusiasm for school has been sustained by enrichment in elementary years will enjoy the flexibility and additional course offerings in grades nine through twelve.

It is wonderful when a teacher or tutor can work on a regular basis with a group of children who share a common interest. If the school's point of view permits, such opportunities can be arranged. Meetings might be scheduled in study hall periods or replace other preordained events. A group of four or five mathematically gifted students, poets, artists, or scientists can accomplish a great deal while having a splendid time. Publishing a school newspaper proved to be just such an opportunity for one multi-aged group of students and a very gifted teacher. He challenged them to produce one whole issue using nothing but advertising, propaganda, and opinion. The students were intrigued by the idea, adored playing with the appropriate language, and were delighted with their end product. (Needless to say, they are all astute propaganda spotters now.)

Extracurricular activities such as art, shop, music, or drama provide an excellent opportunity for the gifted child to develop some of the counterweights mentioned earlier. The child's view of the world becames larger and he increases the number of expressive capabilities at his command. All children need this enrichment, but for the reasons discussed earlier, the gifted child's needs are particularly intense. Ideally, this should be part of the regularly scheduled academic day or week and available to all ages.

Brentwood College of Education in Brentwood, England, was host to an experimental program run by Sidney Bridges and described in *The Gifted Child and the Brentwood Experiment*.[1] Gifted children who attend their regular schools during the week would come to the college on Friday afternoons for special activities. The

[1]S. Bridges, *The Gifted Child and the Brentwood Experiment* (London: Pitman's Educational, 1975).

87

purpose of the project was to provide companionship and intellectual nourishment without interrupting the children's regular lives. The first report of the project states:

> It is to this work that we owe the first unequivocal statement by gifted children that while they loved being with their intellectual peers for part of their week, they would not wish to separate from their own class full-time.[2]

After-school or weekend groups can offer companionship, challenge, variety, and big blocks of time. Participants can work on drama, chess, electronics, art, music—there is no limit to interesting subject matter. A recent brochure describing an independently sponsored Saturday program for gifted children in Westchester County, New York, listed astronomy and celestial navigation, pot gardening, mathematical puzzles, maintenance and repair of common household appliances, magic, and madrigal singing.

The National Association For Gifted Children in London has a successful program of Saturday Clubs. In their words, a Saturday Club is a gathering of children, on a regular basis, most of whom are gifted in one way or another. These groups were started for children needing greater opportunity for self-fulfillment than is normally experienced in their everyday lives. Here is how the current brochure describes their scope and curriculum:

SCOPE OF THE CLUB

This is undoubtedly a real, if indirect, value of the club in the sense that it offers some parents new insights into their own children's needs and into hitherto unrealised ways of meeting them.

It is worth noting, too, that outside professional observation of this experiment during the first year gave rise to encouraging and supportive recommendations for future developments, underlining and strengthening the initial success.

[2]George C. Robb, *Retrospect and Prospect: A British View.* Paper given at World Conference on Gifted Children (London, 1975).

A GOODNESS OF FIT

The Saturday Club is primarily for gifted children needing greater opportunity for self-fulfilment than is normally experienced in their everyday lives. An essential value of this process must lie within activity in the company of their peers. This simple definition, however, poses a dilemma. Should the gifted be separated from their natural associates (siblings at the least) for the occasion of their visit to the Saturday Club? *Can* they be so separated? By what standards or testing procedures are they to be so selected!

The association does not recognise any valid specific test for defining 'giftedness'. Nor is it thought desirable to separate siblings during periods of intense and, hopefully, satisfying self-fulfilment such as is afforded by the Saturday Club.

The membership of the club is therefore open to children generally realised to be in need of 'stretching' to a higher level than normally available to them, *and* their brothers and sisters if accompanying them.

There is currently no test in use, yet experience has shown that between parents' awareness, obvious manifestations of ability, and the naturally selective process of personal interest the resulting balance is about right. Siblings of lower ability do not appear to be any problem in managing the club and are welcomed. So far, without testing or other formality the club has maintained an ability intake higher than average. The age range is from 5 years without an upper limit. In practice this has settled itself at about 14. Children from all types of school attend the Saturday Club, with those from the maintained sector (state schools) greatly in the majority.

CURRICULUM

The range of subjects offered by the club must necessarily vary from time to time with the facilities and staff available, as well as with experience. Nevertheless, the following activities are usually offered:

Art, Crafts, Woodworking, Pottery,
Trampoline, Net & ball games,
Board games, Photography, Drama, Music,
Creative writing, Academic subjects

89

There are no formal work programmes culminating in examinations, nor are particular examinations elsewhere recognised as targets. The activities of the club are largely socially cohesive and aimed at self-fulfilment and interest rather than specific attainment.

Who should lead enrichment groups? The qualifications are the same as they are for teachers—knowledge, curiosity, and openness are of greater value than paper certificates. Teachers may wish to work with advanced students in their particular subjects. Parents, community members, or industries may enjoy serving as mentors and are an extremely valuable resource, heretofore insufficiently tapped. Business organizations and professional people sometimes offer apprenticeships. Interested students with adequate background can apply. In addition, industries, professional people, and citizens with a field of expertise are often willing to teach and supervise specific projects. Individual mentors may want to demonstrate their professional knowledge or they may prefer to share an avocation. The cost of a mentor's services range from high pay, with the cost of the sessions being shared by the participants, to modest or token payment, to volunteer participation. Chapter Seven gives more detailed information.

Summary

Families whose children are required to attend one specific school should systematically figure out what the school does well, which of the child's needs are being met within the school, and which require more attention. Life is easier when the desired balance is born of cooperation between faculty and school.

Families with the luxury of choice may decide whether acceleration, segregation, or enrichment seems most likely to suit a particular child, recognizing that each institution offers its own adaptation and each child will bring to it unique skills and needs.

A Goodness of Fit

As soon as the rigid concept of the one perfect program, the one perfect school, or the one perfect gifted child is abandoned, the way is clear for flexible teachers and families to create a goodness of fit between the child and his education.

PART III

What Else They Need

For balanced growth the gifted child needs things to do alone, things to do as a member of a group, and wide exposure to stories and language.

The following suggestions are intended to provide supplementary, not primary, fare. It is important to include the old favorites along with the new ideas because omitting them might seem to denigrate their importance. Also, a familiar idea in an unexpected context can often be the catalyst for an original thought.

Do not treat these next three chapters as a Cordon Bleu recipe in which every ingredient must be used. Rather, use them as you would a menu in a Chinese restaurant, choosing appetizing offerings from categories A, B, and C. Here is a browsing ground for those who plan for gifted children: teachers, parents, community leaders—and the children themselves.

Chapter 6

Solo Activities

Why are they necessary and why is it difficult to provide them?

The gifted child's extra energy needs outlets, opportunities, and channels. When people around him are tired out, he needs things he can do on his own so others can rest without feeling guilty.

Creativity and fine soup have much in common. Really good soup is made up of a principal ingredient, a blend of seasonings to enhance the flavors, and liquid to put the various flavors in touch with one another. Here is how the best cook I know makes her famous turkey soup. She starts with the Thanksgiving carcass, which goes into a heavy pot with water, carrots, celery, onion, thyme, salt, an pepper. Once it has come to a boil and been skimmed, she lets it simmer overnight. By morning the taste and bouquet have been doubled, as the volume has been reduced by half. A long simmer in a securely lidded container produces better soup than a vigorous, short boil with lots of opening and looking. As warmth, privacy, and time are preconditions for soup, so they are, too, for creativity.

WHAT ELSE THEY NEED

At the World Conference on Gifted Children in London in 1975, A. H. Passow, Columbia University professor of education, explored four recognizable phases of creativity. While it may seem inappropriate to chart something as mysterious as creativity, these four steps are well worth considering.

1). preparation
2). incubation
3). illumination
4). verification

The first and the last depend on the outside world. The third comes unbidden and cannot be scheduled or prearranged. Incubation requires soup-pot privacy.

Why is it hard for gifted children to find privacy? Physical limitations of time and space are factors, and also an insidious adult weakness. Many adults are not comfortable in their own company. They fear solitude and fill their time with activities that guarantee companionship. Most little children, and particularly gifted children, do not start out with this fear. They know how to have a wonderful time by themselves. But the adult who hates solitude himself feels guilty watching a child play alone, and intrudes on his privacy with suggestions, conversations, and interruptions. Thus, adult inadequacy robs the child of the chance to enjoy a natural gift.

Here are some activities a child can pursue on his own, with indications of what I would consider appropriate ages where necessary. They will be divided into three categories in an attempt to avoid the pitfall of the endless list.

I. incorporative
II. associative
III. generative

96

SOLO ACTIVITIES

I. Incorporative Activities

Incorporative is a word with several meanings. The *American College Dictionary* gives three: to suck up or drink in, to engross wholly, and to take in without echo or recoil. Here are five incorporative activities.

1. *Reading* is the obvious first. A reader can acquire factual information independently, find out how to do almost anything, and have unlimited aesthetic nourishment. Most gifted children like to read, are willing to try different kinds of stories, and move easily from fiction to fact. Since Chapter Eight is devoted to literature and the gifted child, this space will focus on more factual reading.

All children like having their own magazine subscription. Here are some which gifted children, among others, enjoy. Young children roughly from the ages of four to ten enjoy *Highlights for Children,* 2300 W. Fifth Ave., P. O. Box 269, Columbus, Ohio 43216. Each issue contains things to do as well as stories and features and the magazine received a Certificate of Merit from The National Association for Gifted Children. The child who has outgrown *Highlights* will be ready for *World*, published by the National Geographic (National Geographic World, Dept. 00278, 17th and M Sts. N.W., Washington, D.C. 20036). This is beautifully laid out, with a balance of text, photography, trompe l'oeil, suggested activities, and a regular feature titled "Kids Did It." It is published monthly and a year's subscription costs $5.85. Children from roughly eight to adult enjoy it. For children from roughly ten and up there is a magazine called *Games*, which features puzzles, games, contests, self-tests, and brainteasers. A year's subscription costs $5.97 and the address is P. O. Box 10147, Des Moines, Iowa 50349. For the older child, or the sophisticated mathematician, *Scientific American,* P. O. Box 5919, New York, N.Y. 10001, will provide information, challenge, and delight. If the gifted child in

97

your care has a particular interest—astronomy, computers, motorcycles, or basketweaving—browse through a magazine store or the nearest public library. There are periodicals for nearly every subject. Not only are the articles informative, but nearly all special interest magazines have classified sections announcing both products and upcoming events.

Gifted children need frequent reassurance that they are like other human beings and that we all share common physiology and surroundings. They, like other children, like to understand their bodies. For this I recommend the *Brown Paper School Books*, published by Little, Brown for elementary school children. Here are their eight current titles:

1. *Blood and Guts*
2. *I Am Not a Short Adult*
3. *Everybody's a Winner*
4. *My Backyard History Book*
5. *The I Hate Mathematics Book*
6. *The Book of Think*
7. *The Reason for Seasons*
8. *The Night Sky Book*

Little, Brown also publishes *The Great Perpetual Learning Machine*, a book that overflows and defies categories. It is a collection of thoughts, projects, and puzzles for children alone or in groups.

The teenage gifted child who wants to expand a special mechanical or mathematical interest through independent study should investigate International Correspondence Schools, Scranton, Pa. 18515. They will send a catalogue on request which lists such selections as electrical engineering, electronics, drafting, chemical engineering, surveying and mapping, and house planning and design.

The local librarian is a valuable friend for the gifted child. He or she can show the child how to find materials in a special field of interest, and explain the mysteries of card catalogues and stacks.

The child should also be shown how to keep his own card catalogue. The gifted child, in all likelihood, will read widely, and, delighting as he does in associations and patterns, will cross reference in an unusual way. A card file can help him retrieve information quickly and accurately. Children from roughly the age of eight learn to do this with precision and pleasure. They enjoy the mechanical skills of alphabetizing, using bibliographical form, and categorizing.

It is important to remember that not all independent reading must be of high intellectual caliber. The gifted child needs surcease, occasional nostalgia, and current jokes. He may need to relax with his reading in the same way some of the children in Chapter Four needed to relax with their friends. *Mad* magazine may sometimes be more appropriate than masterworks.

Reading, valuable as it is, is not the only path to knowledge, however.

2. *Television,* our cultural whipping boy, offers some exciting material. Many presentations are appropriate for gifted children. The trick lies in choosing what to watch. Here is a system which works well and requires decision making, evaluation, and thinking, things that television theoretically deadens. When the weekly paper or monthly guide arrives, ask the child to sit down and read it, or read it with him if he is too young to do it alone. Then ask him to circle in red Magic Marker whatever shows he thinks would be good and would fit the family time allowance for television. Go over the choices with him, encouraging him to explain his reasons, discuss the difference between various programs offered simultaneously, and see the patterns and balance of what he has chosen for a week. Invite his predictions of what the various shows will be like, and be sure to listen to his opinions afterwards if you do not, or cannot, watch the program with him. As an example, here is what one nimble-witted ten-year-old boy chose for a week in July—a season when the offered fare is thought to be so thin.

WHAT ELSE THEY NEED

Sunday: 7:00 P.M. *The Hardy Boys and Nancy Drew.*

Before and after comments: "I like mysteries." "I always know they'll get out OK, but I still always get scared in the middle. It's like not being sure even though you really know."

8:00 P.M. *Evening at Pops,* Arthur Fiedler and the Boston Pops with Henry Mancini.

Before and after comments: "I like the way they play. They put surprises in—like the way they play the Rudolph the Red-Nosed Reindeer part in that Christmas record." "Hey—he's the Pink Panther guy!"

Monday: 7:00 P.M. *The Brady Bunch.*

Before and after comments: "Can Sam come over and watch it with me?" "It wasn't bad."

7:30 P.M. *The Muppets.*

Before and after comments: "I love that show." "I love that show."

Tuesday: 8:00 P.M. *West Side Story.*

Before and after comments: "It's hard to choose. There's a National Geographic show, and they're usually good, and there's baseball. I'll choose this because I have the record." "It was good. I love that 'Hey Officer Krupke' song. I wonder who won the ballgame."

Wednesday: 6:30 P.M. *I Love Lucy.*

Before and after comments: "Sometimes I just like to watch something dumb." "It was funny—dumb, but funny."

8:00 P.M. *Nova.*

Before and after comments: "They have good stuff." "Do you think that's true, about people affecting plants? I never thought about that before. In a way it's creepy. I think I'll try."

100

Solo Activities

Thursday: 7:30 P.M. *In Search of Hypnosis.*

Before and after comments: "Maybe I can learn how to hypnotize *you.*" "I'm glad you can't be hypnotized if you don't want to be."

8:00 P.M. *World: Three Days in Szczecin.*

Before and after comments: "Is Poland a free country?" "What happens to people in our country who go on strike?"

Friday: 6:00 P.M. *Zoom.*

Before and after comments: "I like seeing other kids on TV." "I liked it. You know what was funny—the younger kids were better than the older kids. They never looked embarrassed."

8:00 P.M. *Baseball.*

Before and after comments. "Tonight's going to be a good night." "I know what went wrong. They shouldn't have changed pitchers when they did."

Saturday: 7:30 P.M. *The Price is Right.*

Before and after comments: "I like to know how much things cost." "How old do you have to be to get on that show?"

8:00 P.M. *Great Performances,* The Berlin Philharmonic.
Before and after comments: "I love that music." "I don't watch the screen much. I mostly just listen."

Television can be used as an awakener instead of an anaesthetic, as this ten-year-old child clearly demonstrated. Others in his family use it in much the same way. His mother frequently watches *Sunrise Semester,* college courses taught by the faculty of New York University, and his older brother and father, excellent tennis players themselves, like to watch televised tennis matches. Although it is intellectually fashionable to scorn television, it is snobbery to assume that high availability automatically indicates low quality. Rejecting the offerings of a whole medium because

101

some of the selections are poor is throwing out the baby with the bathwater.

3. *Radio.* The same comments and system apply to radio. For the gifted child who is a music lover, classical or contemporary, a good radio is an invaluable companion. Consult your local newspaper for program selections and look ahead to see what's coming. For lovers of classical music, *Musica,* Box 1266, Edison, N.J., lists a thousand AM and FM stations in the United States alphabetically according to state and city, and gives the days and hours of concerts. It costs $3.95 plus 75 cents postage.

Children who enjoy mystery stories should try *Radio Mystery Theater.* Time and station vary regionally.

As with television, shopping through the schedule, choosing, contrasting, and evaluating add an extra dimension to listening which the gifted child welcomes. And, as noted with respect to friends, activities, and reading, sometimes the gifted child needs blandness and surcease.

4. *Puzzles* come in many forms. Gifted children who enjoy visual puzzles will spend happy hours working to assemble jigsaw or three-dimensional-object puzzles or using elastic bands and a geoboard to duplicate complicated printed patterns. This is both a visual and a mathematical puzzle, one of the many possibilities for those who enjoy playing mathematical games and meeting mathematical challenges. Bookstores carry those that are currently popular and generally available. In addition, there is an excellent selection in a catalogue published by Creative Publications, 3977 East Bayshore Rd., P.O. Box 10328, Palo Alto, California 94303. The catalogue itself is a thing of beauty. The books of mathematical puzzles and games of strategy, probability, and pattern are appropriate for groups as well as individuals; detailed descriptions of several are found in Chapter Seven.

The electronic age and miniaturization have given us a host of quiet individual games to be played with calculators, computers, and on television screens. The Creative Publications catalogue offers games for children from grades four and up to play with pocket calculators. The computer games of *Chess Challenger, Checker Challenger,* and *Gammonmaster* Backgammon can be tested and purchased at good-sized camera stores. If $300 is within the family budget of a gifted child who enjoys chess, *Boris,* the portable chess computer, is available. Hand-eye coordination games of television screen handball, tennis, and hockey can be bought at television stores, or at much lower cost at a toy store, under the name Telstar.

Children who enjoy paper and pencil puzzles will enjoy and learn from paperback puzzle books in four series published by Lee Publications, 815–25 E. Market St., Louisville, Ky. 40232: *Yes and Know, Game Books, Guess and Show,* and *Cross and Know.* The answers are printed in invisible ink, which appears when the *Yes and Know* pen (included) is used.

Dover Publications has an excellent book of *Storybook Mazes* which offer a maze accompaniment to each of the fairy tales in the collection. Bookstores generally carry a large selection of books of mazes. *Altair Design* books provide opportunity for original design.

Older gifted children may happily tackle double crostics or crossword puzzles such as those found in the *New York Times.* In fact, one student at an independent school in New York City developed such skill that he taught a course in crossword puzzles at the New School for Social Research in New York.

5. *Collections.* The gifted child, delighting as he does in patterns, cross references, and combinations, may become intrigued by collecting. Here is unlimited opportunity for investigating, searching, categorizing, trading, and displaying. Although the term *collector's item* calls to mind black tie affairs, glass cases, limousines, and Limoges, it needn't be limited to that. Collections can contain things that nature provides free to the finder, things

that must be bought, things that are of current popular interest, or things that are alive. Here are some specifics.

Rocks or leaves make interesting collections and are available for the picking. The country child need only step outside his door. The city child can either go to the country on a day excursion, or simply go to the park. The child who is interested in rocks will find *Rocks and Minerals,* a Golden Press Nature Guide, $1.95, a good book to begin with. The child who wants to collect leaves will find *Trees,* in the same series, helpful. A leaf collection requires the further step of pressing and drying, a learning process in itself. For the child who has access to the seashore, a shell collection is a natural. Two splendid books for identifying shells and marine life are *Seashells of the World,* in the Golden Press Nature Guide Series, and *The Sea Beach at Ebb Tide* by Augusta F. Arnold, published by Dover Publications.

Once the category has been chosen and the collection begun, the young collector must decide how to display it, how to label the various components, and how far to expand it. Box lids can be divided into compartments with cardboard strips and Scotch tape. They can be lined with adhesive-backed paper, in any pattern from marble to gingham, to make effective display cases and can be covered with a layer of plastic wrap to protect the contents.

The Styrofoam packing boxes used for such things as jelly jars are already compartmentalized and can usually be obtained without cost by asking for them at a specialty food shop or supermarket with a gourmet section. If a modest financial outlay is appropriate, go to the hardware store and buy one of the small metal chests of compartmentalized drawers used to keep screws, nails, nuts, washers, and bolts. They make ideal holders for small items and each species can have its own spot and its own label.

If the child is in a position to spend money for collecting, he might enjoy stamps or coins. Each of these has an enthusiastic cadre; there are bulletins, clubs, magazines, and meetings devoted to the subject. For specific local information, check the Yellow Pages of the telephone book under the headings coins, stamps, and hobbies. It is easy to start one of these collections with a modest outlay; it is expensive to expand it as far as the imagination of the gifted child would like to take it.

Two gifted children I know like to collect things of current popular interest. Franklin, who is ten years old, has an enormous collection of baseball cards which he keeps in four shoeboxes and one plastic album the size of a looseleaf notebook. Each album page has twelve see-through pockets per side, designed specifically for baseball cards. He loves to change it around, sometimes arranging his album pages by teams, sometimes by positions and men who play them, or sometimes by the size and weight of the players. He is constantly sorting, shifting, and recategorizing. Today's front page pitcher may find himself in a shoebox tomorrow. Franklin spends contented hours with his collection learning facts, playing with combinations, and according to his taste of the moment, bestowing honor or exile.

Another child, who is also ten, collects commercials and advertising slogans. She has a huge bulletin board on which she tacks those that catch her eye. She has a good ear for music and mimicry and has tape recorded a thirty-minute original medley of commercials beginning with "I Love New York" and ending, "Pop-pop, fizz–fizz, oh what a relief it is—this tape is over." She used considerable skill putting them together and the result sounds almost like a Gilbert and Sullivan patter song.

The gifted child who lacks an opportunity for caretaking may find satisfaction as well as interest in a collection of such live things as tropical fish or plants. His need to be a giver of nurture as well as a receiver of care is powerful and he can take emotional nourishment from such an experience.

Here is a way to begin which works well. Find a good-sized pet shop and go there with the child, a notebook, and a pencil. Look at

105

all the possibilities, write down the necessary equipment, cost, and space required for each, and go home. Away from the seductive appeal of a glistening tank, bubbling water, and darting fish, or the wistful look in the homeless hamster's eye, the child will find it easier to evaluate the alternatives and make his decision. He may decide he'd rather grow varying species of herbs and violets than clean out a cage every day. Then set aside whatever physical space will be required, arrange the financing, whether through loan or piggy bank, and finally, having done the planning, return to the store to make the purchase.

Whatever the category, a collection can provide hours of solitary enjoyment, intellectual nourishment, and sometimes even a dignified new word; there is weight in ichthyologist, numismatist, and philatelist.

II. Associative Activities

Associative activities encourage the child's natural proclivity for playing with analogy. His whole world teases him with its attributes, as he finds ways to combine the new with the already familiar or to put familiar things together in novel partnerships. Here are four such activities.

The first is a book for the child to write about himself. As a teacher, I have used this with reading-disabled children who had never before found anything very interesting in the printed word. I have also used it with extremely able, imaginative children who wanted to soar.

In writing this book, the child forges a three-link chain connecting the written word, the world around him, and himself. It offers infinite opportunities for original thinking and, once begun, will be read and reread, for children, like adults, enjoy reading about themselves. Here is how to set up ten pages.

106

Page 1 is about the child's birthday. At the top write the old rhyme.

> Monday's child is fair of face.
> Tuesday's child is full of grace.
> Wednesday's child is full of woe.
> Thursday's child has far to go.
> Friday's child is loving and giving.
> Saturday's child must work for a living.
> The child born on the Sabbath Day
> > Is blithe and bonny, merry and gay.

At the bottom write a line that says, "I am a _____ child." In case the poor child is a Wednesday, Thursday, or Saturday child, conclude with a line that says, "I do/do not believe this old poem."

Page 2 shows the child how to find his place in the Chinese calendar. It says, "The Chinese calendar names years for animals. The calendar is on a 12-year cycle. Here are some recent years. Now you can figure out your own year: 1977, Dragon; 1976, Rabbit; 1975, Tiger; 1974, Ox; 1973, Rat; 1972, Pig; 1971, Dog; 1970, Rooster; 1969, Monkey; 1968, Sheep; 1967, Horse; 1966, Snake." End with a line that says, "I was born in the year of the _____ ." Add as much interpretation of these animals' characteristics as the child enjoys.

Page 3 does the same thing with zodiac information. A current horoscope column from your local newspaper adds zest.

Page 4 is about the child's name and says, "This is my name in code." There are spaces for him to write his name in Morse Code, semaphore or nautical flag code, a code substituting numbers for letters, and finally, a space for him to write in code a word he likes to use in describing himself. Morse Code and semaphore can be found in an encyclopedia and the substitution code can be an original invention.

Page 5 says, "When I go out to buy clothes, I like to _____, but

I hate to _____," and "When I get up on Saturday morning, I like to put on _____ and this is how I look [illustration]."

Page 6 provides an opportunity to put dislikes and unpleasant things on paper. Many children are surprised that this is permissible. For them, this page opens up a whole new world. For others, it is just plain fun. It says:

> I do not like to eat _____.
> I do not like to wear _____.
> I do not like to go to _____.
> I do not like to listen to _____.
> I do not like to see _____.
> I do not like the feeling of _____.
> I hope I never have to _____ again.

Be sure to make the blank spaces big enough to accommodate lots of ideas.

Page 7 is called "Bon Appetit." It says: "My favorite breakfast is _____; my favorite lunch is _____; my favorite snack is _____. My mother says _____ is bellywash, but I love it."

Page 8 is titled "Initial Reactions," and says, "Write your initials in the space below. Now choose descriptive words that start with these initials, and you will have a new name."

Page 9 is called "Here I Go." It says, "Write Yes or No: I slither _____, I crawl _____, I tiptoe _____," and so forth. Other verbs I have used are march, dance, wobble, gyrate, cavort, wiggle, vacillate, twist, and perambulate.

Page 10 uses the same yes or no format and is called "I Do, I Do." It says: "I lacerate, recount, verbalize, embellish, blush, respirate, imagine, create, tease, exacerbate, exaggerate. I bring joy!"

Should you want samples and suggestions for other pages, you will find them in *Supplement to a Teacher's Notebook: Alternatives for Children with Learning Problems* by Migdail and Vail, published by the National Association of Independent Schools, 4 Liberty

Square, Boston, Mass. 02109, $2.00. It includes a section on storywriting which the gifted have used in particularly imaginative ways. Most children are usually eager to think up ideas for many new pages on their own.

The second suggestion is *Treasure Hunt,* an open-ended, noncompetitive game which provides hours of enjoyment. It can be played by a group or by one child alone. Choose any one of the thousands of shapes and patterns that surround us. Circles and symmetry are two examples. Listing them by word, or simple drawing, the child discovers where and how frequently the chosen pattern can be found. His whole world is the hunting ground. For example, consider how many circles a careful observer could find in the kitchen, or how much symmetry is in human bodies, plants, flowers, shells, architecture, and design, from the chassis of an automobile to the grapefruit display at the supermarket. Keeping track is entertaining and finding shapes or patterns in unexpected places provides a thrill of surprise. The Creative Publications catalogue mentioned earlier uses *Math in Nature* as its design theme. The results are surprising and lovely.

The third suggestion is drawing while listening to music, which can produce surprising results. Sometimes it is more fun to draw to many different pieces and kinds of music. Another kind of fun lies in hearing the same piece five or six times and drawing something different from each hearing. Contrasting the results with one another is an intriguing way to interpret mood and association. Most children are not reluctant to draw unless their natural willingness has been extinguished by a rigid art program in school, or by adult mockery.

The fourth is category albums, or collages. They are entertaining to make and can be unusual and eye-catching. The child needs paper, scissors, paste, and a stack of old magazines and catalogues. A category can be suggested in advance and adhered to, or an older child may delight in keeping the category secret, making the collage or album, and challenging others to find the common denominator.

The fifth suggestion is tricks. Chapter Seven has specific suggestions about magic, which the gifted child can learn and practice alone or in a group. Here is another suggestion particularly appropriate to the child who is alone at bedtime or in the evening, *Hand Shadows to Be Thrown Upon the Wall: A Series of Novel andAmusing Figures Formed by the Hand* by Henry Bursill, Dover Publications.

Dover Publications has a comprehensive group of books which teach tricks. They are inexpensive and the directions are clear.

III. Generative Activities

Generative activities are those that result in a specific product. Why are they important? Think in the imagery of pipes and water tanks. The gifted child has huge equipment for taking in. It is as though his pipes are many and of a very wide diameter. He needs many pipes leading out, and a generous supply of faucets, to prevent a flood or an explosion. Generative activities turn on the faucets.

There is another value which must not be overlooked. They give the child an additional way to meet a world not always friendly to him. Jealousy and fear often generate resentment of a gifted child. The brilliant mathematician or the satiric poet may frighten many people. But his home-baked brownies, a lovely piece of needlework, or a musical rendition doesn't. And a slight detectable flaw (a good possibility in cooking, sewing, or instrument playing) makes the creator seem more human rather than less, a welcome shift for the gifted child.

Nine specific generative activities follow.

110

SOLO ACTIVITIES

1. *Playing a musical instrument.* The joy and nourishment of music has been described through the ages. If a gifted child is musically inclined, have plenty of time for him to play and practice. If he is interested but doesn't know how to play, try to provide an introductory series of lessons. While he is still experimenting, rent his instrument instead of buying it. That will give him more leeway and allow him to try several, if need be, before deciding on one. If he already knows how to play, and enjoys ensembles, explore the series of records titled *Music Minus One*, published and packaged by Music Minus One, 43 West 61 St., New York, N.Y. 10023. These are available for almost every instrument, and go from beginning to advanced levels.

2. *Drawing, painting, or sculpting.* As with music, if the child is already skillful, give him time and privacy. If he is interested but hasn't yet chosen a medium, go with him to an art store, and let him browse through their introductory level materials. Here are some typical offerings.

For the child who would like to try sculpture, Caran d'Ache has a set of ten blocks of perpetually soft colored clay for $10.80. *Paris Craft,* an instant papier mâché, is available for $4.00

For the very young painter, there is an excellent item by Talens called Poster Blocks. These are large blocks of tempera paints which come in a set of six for $8.95. Since the blocks are big, the children can use big brushes, which are better suited to little hands than the tiny brushes usually found in watercolor sets. Acrylic paints can be used on anything, paper, cardboard, glass, or even stones. A modular set can be bought for $8.00.

The child who would like to draw but doesn't know quite how to start should look at the Grumbacher series in which my favorite is *The Art of Drawing Animals.* (This series can be found in any art store or hobby shop.) For $5.00 the child gets a book, paper, four pencils, a sharpener, an eraser, and two smudgers. A child who wants less instruction might buy a beginner's drawing set. A typi-

111

cal one contains five pencils differing in hue and hardness, erasers, and smudgers and costs $7.25.

3. *Athletics*—practicing and polishing an athletic skill: skating, gymnastics, dance, shooting baskets, or whatever the child particularly likes. Since so much depends on whether the child lives in the city or the country, what facilities are close enough for him to reach on his own, and what his personal inclinations are, I will simply mention the category and not try to be specific.

4. *Writing.* The gifted child needs many opportunities to express himself. Writing is an ideal one. It can take the form of original poetry, stories, plays, or a journal. Or he may enjoy copying some favorite selections and illustrating them or illuminating the first letter of each line. An ideal vessel is the blank books now available at stationery stores or counters for roughly $4.00. They come with attractive covers, they look like real books, but the pages are blank.

5. *Building:* models, dioramas, electronic wonders, collages. The purpose can be aesthetic delight, historical accuracy, precision, scientific knowledge, experimentation, or any combination of the above.

Take the child who is interested in building models to a hobby shop rather than to the plastic model department of a discount store for this reason. It is very hard to assess the level of manual dexterity required simply by looking at the picture on a box. Discouragement and frustration result when a goodness of fit is lacking between the child's skill and the agility required. A good hobby shop will give reliable recommendations. Logix-kosmos has a science experiment set called *Electronics* in which the child first builds a console, and then through building increasingly complicated circuits learns how to make such things as a lie detector, automatic light switch, and two-transistor radio. This is available at toy stores. If a doll house has greater appeal than a police siren, try *All About Doll Houses*, published by Bobbs Merrill.

Don't forget Lego, which, although initially expensive, is beautifully made, lasts forever, has intriguing components, and can be used to make almost anything. A gifted child can spend hours imagining and creating.

6. *Cooking.* Whether the palate inclines to vegetarian fare, soups, crepes, Chinese, Mexican, German, French, or down-home food, there is a cookbook. A word of caution: many cookbooks written for children have bland or sugary foods with such whimsical labels as Red Riding Hood's Applesauce or Seven Dwarf Cookies. The gifted child is usually well able to enjoy and prepare more sophisticated and nutritious offerings. Bypass the junior cookbooks and go instead to such specialties as quiches or Chinese cooking. With a little help and experience, the gifted child will find his favorite toy—patterns—and understand why certain ingredients are necessary and how they work together. He will understand intellectually as well as enjoy gastronomically.

7. *Gardening.* Since so much depends on where the gifted child lives, this is hard to describe in detail. However, there are two cardinal rules: keep it small, and insure success. The country child who is given a six-by-six-foot plot of earth and six packages of seed from the hardware store has more than a beginner can manage and will be turned away for life. Little children like to garden in little pots. Hanging shelves for window gardening are inexpensive, available at garden supply shops, and keep the project in one location. One such garden, planned and tended by a nine-year-old girl, had a top shelf with four different kinds of ivy, another with two varieties each of begonia and African violets, and a bottom shelf of herbs which were a mainstay of the family salad bowl. Sprout gardening is quick, tidy, and tasty. Equipment is inexpensive and available in hardware stores, health food stores, and some garden shops. Terrariums give room for a huge variety of species in a small space and they accept but do not require constant attention.

8. *Photography*. Because this is expensive and requires a dark-room, a great deal of equipment, and initial supervision, I simply mention it. The visually acute gifted child whose family has plenty of space and money may find it an ideal occupation and one that will bless them in return with beautiful results.

9. *Handcrafts*. These include sewing, weaving, ceramics, leatherwork, carving, macramé, to name but a few. Mercifully, sex-related cultural taboos are losing their power. Both boys and girls can enjoy all the above. There are five publishers whose handcraft and how-to books are favorites of mine because their directions are clear, their offerings are varied, they are inexpensive, and they encourage the reader to try something that might initially seem difficult. Doubtless there are other fine publications unknown to me which do the same things, but here are my personal preferences.

1. Sunset Hobby and Craft Books
   Lane Publishing Co.
   Menlo Park, California 94025
       sample crafts: Bonsai, leather, macramé, sewing

2. McCall's
       sample title: *Golden Do-It Book*. This offers a wide variety of short, accomplishable projects. Their needlecraft suggestions are particularly well done.

3. Time-Life Encyclopedias.
       sample title: *Gardening Under Lights*

4. Drake Home Craftsman's Books
       sample titles: *Making Toys in Wood, A Woodcarver's Primer, Understanding High Fidelity*

5. Dover Publications
       sample titles: *Fruit and Vegetable, Iron-On Transfer Patterns*, Dover Coloring Books: *Seashore Life, Garden Flowers*, and

so forth. These make excellent embroidery outlines and are a blessing to the craftsperson who delights in using unusual combinations of color, stitchery, or collage, but does not draw well.

Two books that are not part of any series are *The Ashley Book of Knots*, published by Doubleday, and *Sculptured Needlepoint Stitchery* by Ella Projansky (Scribner's). Knots have historical uses, and are practical as well as decorative. Gifted boys and girls enjoy learning their history and associations as well as learning how to make them and for what use each is appropriate. Mrs. Projansky is an accomplished needlewoman who, like a gifted child, delights in novel combinations and unusual patterns. She brings a freewheeling spirit to the geometric grid of canvas. Her book not only shows how to make various stitches but through the examples she gives she teases the reader's imagination and encourages originality.

Once again—a craft does not belong to one sex or the other. Joy in creating something new is for both boys and girls.

If the ideas in this chapter carry out the purpose for which they are listed, they will not be the end of a search, but the beginning of new plans.

Chapter 7

Group Activities

Belonging is a need and right of every gifted child. In early years group activities offer companionship and a place to develop social skills. In adolescence the common bond of group membership provides attachment to the world and feelings of similarity and safety. When a young person's feelings are turbulent and he finds himself changing, sometimes against his own will, he is apt to feel bizarre and unlike anyone else. Already feeling different because he is gifted, he may be unable to bear additional loneliness. Group activities use a natural resource we have on hand: one another. They needn't be expensive or solemn; they should provide enjoyment and tease the imagination.

The gifted child (particularly if he is an only child) needs to know how to belong to a group and not just how to be the leader. Martin is a brilliant man who is now in his late forties. An accomplished student all the way through school, he delighted in scientific knowledge and precision. Although he was ambitious, he was also kind. He enjoyed being a leader and his classmates fell into the habit of electing him class president. In his senior year he was president of the student body. Having the habit of leadership, he spoke with authority and walked with assurance. When he went to college, his classmates again chose him as a leader. After graduation he went steadily to the top in his business life, once again a leader. Yet our compassion should go out to him. He is a man who knows how to lead and control, but not how to participate. He and his wife are master and servant, not partners. His children were obedient when young and now that they have outgrown adolescent rebellion, they are polite to him, but secretive about their thoughts and feelings. Martin is doomed to loneliness even though he is frequently surrounded by people.

The gifted child's need for group activities is particularly intense when school is not in session. Weekends may seem long and summer vacation troublesome unless it is well planned. Whether the child needs help finding ways to pursue a particular passion or ways to broaden or focus his interests, well-planned group activities can provide satisfaction and stimulation. Here are three places to look for them: (1) activities planned particularly for children, (2) the world of travel, and (3) the adult world made accessible to children.

Activities planned particularly for children

ATHLETICS

To be a welcome member of an athletic team is to belong! Fortunate indeed is the gifted child who loves baseball, soccer, hockey or lacrosse. And the well-coordinated boy or girl who enjoys sports but dislikes or fears direct physical contact can still be a team player in such cumulative score games as track, swimming, diving, or skating. The camaraderie of team practice, the interdependence, the shared suspense of the contest, the victory cele-

118

bration, or the joint disappointment are powerful group epoxy. Frequently it is unnecessary to belong to an expensive club to play these sports. For local information consult the recreation department of the town where you live as well as the YMCA, YWCA, Boy's Club, or Girl's Club.

SCOUTING

The quality varies from place to place, but scouting is worth investigating. In well-led troups scouts learn skills and facts together, and many young people enjoy the external membership badge of a uniform. Both the Boy Scouts of America and the Girl Scouts of America are making a conscious effort to expand their programs with more contemporary kinds of community outreach than the stereotyped images of helping old ladies across the street and rubbing two sticks together to make a fire. The vigor of the program depends on the local chapter.

COMMUNITY RESOURCES

Here is what the resources in one medium-sized New England community offered on weekends and during the summer for children between the ages of six and fourteen for fees which averaged $2.00 per hour: children's drama, karate, Chinese cooking, birds and snakes, Who Lives in the Marsh?, astronomy, marine biology, macramé, weaving, pottery, woodworking with hand tools, elementary, intermediate, or advanced electronics, and Houses of New England—history and design.

SATURDAY CLUBS FOR GIFTED CHILDREN

As interest in gifted children grows, these clubs are springing up in many places. If there is one near you, investigate it. If there is

119

not, and you are interested in starting one, here are some experiences, philosophies, and activities to consider.

When they are well run, Saturday Clubs provide stimulation, companionship, new opportunities, and new faces. However, those who are trying to administer or establish them find admissions criteria to be a bundle of burrs. An unpleasant atmosphere seems to creep into those clubs whose admissions policies are designed to exclude rather than include: exit sharing, enter upmanship. Sometimes the struggle to establish the criteria is so difficult that adult energies go into codifying rather than into planning for the children. Here is what happens in one club.

Each candidate must take a battery of tests designed to measure IQ, social maturity, creativity, and also achievement tests in reading and mathematics. In order to qualify for the club the child must score a full-scale IQ of over 125 and be at least two years above grade level in achievement scores. In addition to a personal interview, he must present a letter of recommendation from two teachers. Each family is responsible for writing a history of the child's development and paying for the testing, which, at this writing, is $150. If more than one child in a family wishes to apply, each additional child must go through the same procedure and there is no guarantee that siblings will be accepted. With so much time devoted to deciding who may and may not participate, there are lengthy staff meetings and a disproportionately small number of hours left for actual activities.

Another club in a more rural, less affluent community took a different approach. Instead of starting with admissions policies, they began by planning possible programs. They considered available personnel—teachers, parents, mentors—and decided what subjects they could teach in a manner and tempo suitable for gifted children. In the first semester they offered magic, chess, story writing combined with bookbinding, and choral singing.

They printed a small brochure which they distributed locally, inviting applications. Their admissions criteria were:

1. desire of the applicant himself to join
2. parental belief that the child would enjoy and profit from the pace and level of the activities
3. personal interviews with parent and child together
4. evaluation of results of standardized testing already done by the school which would indicate high aptitude

Brothers or sisters of a participant were welcome as long as they themselves wanted to come. Tuition was set by giving each participant a share of the expenses: a small rental fee for the use of a parish house, a modest fee for materials, and the cost of faculty salaries for teachers, who were paid $8.00 per hour. The program bloomed. New courses were added and new families joined, bringing enthusiasm and ideas with them. At the conclusion of the first year there was an exhibit and a party complete with magic show and group singing in which everyone was invited to join. Some of these participants might have scored less than 125 on an IQ test. They came to no harm in the program. Some children left by choice after three or four sessions because the program was too hard for them. Others, by far the greatest number, found companionship, challenge, and new interests.

Here are some activities other groups have used and which have appealed to children of many different ages. I have sorted them into seven categories but not tried to specify any age or grade level for each since so much depends on the size of the group and the expertise of its members. Most of them are inexpensive, reflecting my belief that enrichment and excitement need not depend on a big bank balance.

1. *Games and activities of strategy, probability, and pattern.* These can be learned and played in groups as small as two or as large as a community of interest. Little expense is involved, and there are

great challenge and hours of enjoyment, as well as opportunity for nonphysical competition. Checkers, chess, *Battleship, Mastermind,* and *Othello* are five well-known examples. Gifted children are frequently afraid to compete because losing is so painful. A few tips such as those in the Dover Press chess and checkers strategy books, *Win at Checkers* by Millard Hopper, for example, could provide a needed boost of confidence. Gifted children are frequently good card players. Teach them to play bridge. A book called *Bridge for Bright Beginners,* Dover Publications, will help you get off the ground. A book with clear descriptions of other card games is *Deal Me In* by Margie Golick, W. W. Norton & Co. Some clubs like to organize tournaments as soon as the children have reached an appropriate skill level. Others find that children prefer to choose their own opponents and dislike the ranking within the group that results from tournament play.

Attribute blocks and the games, puzzles, and activities which accompany them are favorites of all ages. They encourage the child to classify and see logical relationships and they can be used cooperatively as opposed to competitively. Activities start with those suitable for preschool children and continue on to very high levels. The blocks and their companion activities can be purchased in many stores. However, I would suggest ordering them from the catalogue of Creative Publications (3977 East Bayshore Rd., P.O. Box 10328, Palo Alto, California, 94303). The catalogue in itself is an excellent source book for teachers, parents, mathematicians, puzzle addicts, thinkers, and questioners. It is arranged in five sections: Arithmetic, Numbers and Operations, Logical Thinking and Problem Solving, Geometry, Measurement, and finally, Resource Books and Materials.

J. Weston Walsh in Portland, Maine, publishes some excellent and inexpensive books of logic puzzles which are arranged in order of difficulty and are appropriate for elementary school children. *Wiff'n Proof* is a challenge to sophisticated mathematicians, as

122

is Martin Gardner's column of mathematical games in each month's issue of *Scientific American*. Two well-written books are *Mathematical Puzzles for Beginners and Enthusiasts* by Geoffrey Mott-Smith (Dover Publications) and *Math Puzzles and Games* by Michael Holt (Walker and Company). This last not only has mathematical games but contains one chapter on Magic and Party Tricks with Numbers, and another on Illusions. The study of illusion is an ideal preamble or companion to the study of magic.

2. *Magic*. Magic is appropriate for pairs or groups to learn together and a strong bond unites the initiates. It can be limited to the kinds of card tricks and illusionary stunts described in *Math Puzzles and Games* or expanded to handkerchiefs and disappearing coins, or top hats and rabbits. This depends partly on what the group is ready to learn but more importantly on how much the magician/teacher knows how to teach—or is willing to share. If you don't know a magic teacher personally, or can't conjure one up, it is possible to locate one by consulting the Yellow Pages for names of practicing magicians and magicians' supply stores. Children enjoy being shown the same trick simultaneously, practicing up on one another, and fanning out into the world to "astonish family and friends."

3. *Visual puzzles*. The Creative Publications catalogue mentioned earlier advertises some beautiful and challenging visual puzzles, many of which are three dimensional. In particular, the Soma puzzle and its companion book by the mathematician and poet Piet Hein can be bought for $4.50. Children from the age of eight on up can spend hours with it. Also offered is a three-dimensional game of Tic Tac Toe; 3D chess and checkers are available in toy and game stores, but not in this catalogue.

Two-dimensional puzzles include jigsaw puzzles, tangrams, mazes, and geoboards. The latter are a favorite with many children. Geoboard activities, which are companionable for two children at a time, offer an opportunity to study a complicated visual pattern, break it down into components, and reproduce it. They are entertaining and challenging for children from the age of four on up. Some children who are highly gifted visually may enjoy them earlier.

4. *Language activities.*

a. *Nonverbal languages.* Languages other than those spoken in human voices are all around us. How many more things we can understand, and how our own store of expressive capabilities expands, as we learn to understand them! Here are three examples.

A group of children can have a wonderful time learning to interpret and use body English. It is a first cousin to pantomime, which all children enjoy. They love finding out supposed meanings of common body positions. Start with a discussion of what emotions they themselves may be expressing with their own bodies. *The Body Language of Children* by Suzanne Szass (W. W. Norton & Co., 500 Fifth Ave., New York, N.Y. 10036) would make a good beginning. The black and white photographs are perfect illustrations of her text and she describes emotions all of us have shared. Continue from there. Does the group agree, for instance, that crossing your legs away from your conversational partner indicates disagreement or aversion? Children who become fascinated with body English may go into a phase of striking poses which will definitely put a damper on spontaneous socializing; however, it will heighten their appreciation of good acting and perhaps improve their performance in charades.

What do animals mean by their various physical poses? Tail-wagging and purring are the idiom of two domestic animals and we all know what skunks and porcupines do to their enemies. But how many know that one wolf shows submission to another by exposing his throat? Adults who are interested in finding out more on this subject can read *The Question of Animal Awareness* by Donald R. Griffin (Rockefeller University Press, 1230 York Ave., New York, N.Y. 10021) and *Look Who's Talking* by Emily Hahn

124

(T. Y. Crowell, 10 E. 53 St., New York, N.Y. 10022). A card game of matching pose with emotion could go on for hours. Set it up as Old Maid, Rummy, Go Fish, or Concentration. If you want to make such a game order some blank playing cards from Creative Publications. They cost $2.50 for 100 or $8.00 for 400. Make pairs by writing a word naming an emotion on one card, and an illustration of a pose (or verbal description if you cannot draw) on another. To forestall argument make a master card listing possible pairing combinations. Then play the game following the rules of Old Maid, Rummy, or whichever format the group has chosen.

While weather does not actually tell stories, it can be considered a language in that it sends signals we can learn to interpret. For instance, as every sailor and pilot knows, different kinds of clouds herald different weather conditions, as do different winds. Learning to interpret these signals in order to predict what is coming is like being let in on a secret. One Saturday Club for gifted children devoted several months to studying weather—graphing precipitation, wind, temperature, and barometric pressure. As an accompaniment they made a collection of common weather proverbs and tried to discover their probable origins. From "ring around the moon, rain coming soon" to "red sky in the morning, sailors take warning" our folklore is rich with such sayings. It was socially and intellectually entertaining for this group to relate science and old wives' tales.

b. *Foreign languages.* Learning to use and understand a foreign language is a requirement in many schools. A child who is particularly adept may wish to learn additional ones or a child or family going on a trip may want to learn a particular one. But here is a delightful game, not formally academic and not aimed at a specific event, to play with a foreign language and children who are mature enough to understand onomatopoeia.

The person in charge chooses a selection written in another language. He reads it aloud if his pronunciation is good, or plays it

125

from a recording. Each participant listens to it, and from the sounds decides what he thinks it is about and writes out a short translation. Almost always each person has a different interpretation. One teacher read a selection in German to a group of eight students. One thought it was about the moon, one thought it was about a naughty child, one a storm at sea, one a flower garden, and one a hibernating bear. Another thought it was the words to a lullabye and two people thought it had to do with machinery. It turned out to be an insurance policy. Once the truth was revealed the selection was read again and the participants talked about which words and sounds had led them to their various conclusions.

c. *Codes* provide privacy and delight. Use Morse Code, nautical flag code, hieroglyphic code, codes made by substituting numbers for letters or letters for one another. Cryptography appeals to all ages, is available for all levels, and joins the initiates together in a shared secret. A good book for elementary school children to begin with is *Spycraft*, published by Scholastic.

Indian Sign Language by William Tomkins (Dover Publications) provides a clear explanation and illustrations of pictography and sign language and, using short selections, gives simple directions on how to comprehend and transmit words, phrases, and complete sentences. This would be an appropriate companion or extension of code study, a subject likely to have strong appeal for fifth and sixth graders who like to be keepers of hidden mysteries.

d. *Nuances.* One group of gifted eleven- and twelve-year-olds studied the various languages found in newspapers, travel folders, fund-raising appeals, and other printed materials that surround us daily. They learned to distinguish among propaganda, advertising, fact, and opinion. After they had learned to notice these, they practiced using them on one another by inventing new products and deciding what kind of language to use to advertise and sell them. One boy invented a mythical cream called Acni-way, reputed to improve the complexions and social prospects of adolescents afflicted with pimples. He designed a label incorporating before and after caricatures, wrote a jingle using the advertising techniques he had been studying, and promised a free sample to each classmate who would use the cream and write a testimonial. He and his friends never passed a cosmetics counter again with their previous degree of gullibility.

e. *Radio and television.* Remember the caveats in the last chapter on selection and snobbery. Both media offer programs which can teach a great deal to a group, particularly if they are discussed before and after listening to them. Here is one way. Choose a program. Listen to it or watch it together as a group. At the conclusion each group member picks words to describe some element, perhaps the villain. Chart how many words appeared on every person's list. How many appeared only once? Try to think of another person who could be described by these same words. Use the same exercise to describe additional characters, types of plot, different moods, settings, costumes, or subjective evaluations. The opportunities are endless. If each participant tries to choose unusual words instead of obvious ones, the vocabulary will be rich.

Or interpret through crafts instead of words. After a group of seven-year-old children heard a description of different kinds of islands, each child was given a shirt cardboard, some paints, clay, and papier mâché and asked to design his own island. Each child had been given a little booklet in which to write a description of the island's location, climate, vegetation, population, greatest problem, and greatest treasure. Each creation was unique and each child adored seeing what his friends had imagined. The culmination was a reading of *The Bad Island* by William Steig.

Essence, the *Dictionary Game,* and *Botticelli* are old-fashioned parlor games familiar to those of us who grew up in a pretelevision era. Like *Charades* and *The Game* they can be played by

127

young and old together as well as chronologically matched groups.

Essence—a personality-analogy game. Start with four or five public figures whose personalities and occupations are very different from one another. Make a chart or booklet about each one listing such facts as age, birthplace, career, successes, obstacles, failures, favorite sports, hobbies, and favorite foods. Be sure to include some pictures. As the group develops these profiles they will come to know the people well. Then play the game this way. One player chooses one of the five public figures but does not say which one. The others try to figure out the identity by asking such questions as, "If he were a color, what color would he be?" "If he were a plant, what kind of plant would he be?" The point is not to use colors or plants which the character owns, but rather those that express the essence of his personality. One game with ten women characters and ten children went this way:

Q. If she were a color, what color would she be?
A. An orangey-red.
Q. If she were a snack, what would she be?
A. Watercress sandwiches on very thin whole wheat bread, vintage champagne, and fresh strawberries.
Q. If she were a book, what kind of book would she be?
A. A slender volume of poetry, bound in blue leather.
Q. If she were a sport, what sport would she be?
A. Badminton.
Q. If she were a body of water, what kind would she be?
A. Fast-moving stream in the mountains with fish and occasional deep, quiet pools.
A. I know! I know! Katharine Hepburn.

Young children cannot play this game because they get stuck on possessions. When asked what color best represents the character, they will give the color of the dress she is wearing in the picture, or say "blackish" about every man who wears a suit. But once the group catches on to extrapolation and symbolism, there is no end. Continue adding to the central supply of characters, being sure that each member of the group knows who the possibilities are and has some idea what each is like.

For older children or people who share a common knowledge of characters, the preliminary steps are unnecessary. They are suggested to keep an inexperienced player from choosing his grandmother, whom no one else knows. The children may want to use one another, but before allowing it, the teacher must be sure they will be able to carry it off without hurting anyone's feelings by using accurate but unflattering analogies.

The Dictionary Game—a game of definitions. The person who is "it" chooses a word from the dictionary—the more abstruse the better. Other players listen, consider, then write out what sounds to them like a logical definition. "It" writes out the actual definition and adds it to the collection. The person who is "it" reads all the definitions aloud once, then rereads each one aloud and asks for a vote. Players vote for the definition they think is the real one. The player whose bogus definition gets the most points is the winner and either he or the player who guesses the actual definition chooses the next word.

Botticelli—an associative guessing game appropriate for players who share a common cultural knowledge. In general I have found that while this game angers children younger than seventh grade, it is apt to cause an epidemic in high school. The person who is "it" chooses a character, real or fictional, living or dead, and tells the other players the first letter of the character's last name. Other players try to guess the identity of the character by asking indirect identity questions of "it" which he must answer by furnishing the name of still another character with the same initial. Thus, if "it" chooses to be Romeo he would simply say R. Play might proceed thus:

WHAT ELSE THEY NEED

Q. Are you a Russian composer?
A. No, I am not Rachmaninoff.
Q. Are you a baseball player?
A. No, I am not Babe Ruth.
Q. Are you a cowboy?

The questioner must have a specific person in mind before asking his question. In other words he himself must know a cowboy whose last name begins with R. If "it" is stumped by the last question and is unable to come up with Roy Rogers he must give a direct answer to a factual question such as "Are you male or female?" To make the game harder the direct questions can be limited to yes or no questions. To make it more elastic, allow such questions as "Where do you live?" If "it" thinks his interrogator is bluffing and does not, for instance, know a cowboy whose name begins with R he may challenge. He receives one immunity from a direct question for each successful challenge, and must answer one direct question for each unsuccessful challenge. The game ends when Romeo is discovered and the player who discovered the truth is the next "it."

Charades and *The Game* are games of pantomime in which "it" acts out a word by syllables, or acts out whole phrases, titles, or slogans. In *Charades* the goal is to be obscure and make it as hard as possible for the opposition to guess. In *The Game* the goal is to help one's team guess the words as quickly as possible. Though local rules vary as to what hints and how many hints are permissible, there is a common agreement that the actor may not speak.

Scrabble, Boggle, and *Wordsworth*, a verbal cousin to *Mastermind,* are three well-designed games which challenge adults as well as young players. For additional ideas consult *The Mammoth Book of Word Games,* Hart Publishing Co., and *The Book of Think* along with the other titles in the Brown Paper School Book series pub-

130

lished by Little, Brown and designed for children and grown-ups to use together.

5. *Brainstorming and simulation.*

Brainstorming. Questions with no known correct asnwer will delight the divergent thinker. Here are three questions that have been used over and over, and reappear by popular demand.

What if?
Where did?
What will?

"What if the sun never set" can lead to a discussion of:

1. Problems of agriculture and world food supply.
2. People's natural rhythms for working, eating, and sleeping. Is jet lag a myth?
3. How do people behave when they do not have enough sleep?
4. What is the role of nocturnal animals?
5. How diurnal and nocturnal animals share the same territory.
6. The use poets, painters, and philosophers have made of dawn and sunset.
7. Different summer and winter behaviors of people who live in high latitudes.

Other good discussion starters are: "Where did . . . the world get rocks?" and "What will . . . food be in the year 2050?" The participating children themselves will come up with many more.

The answers seem to settle into three categories: probable, possible, and mythical. This can lead the way to finding and reading different cultures' mythical responses to these same questions. Once the children have played with the ideas themselves they will take special delight in other people's thoughts.

Simulation games. One of the most exciting and successful simulation games I have ever seen was invented and led by John Fennell, a gifted teacher in Bedford, New York. Working in school with a group of roughly one hundred fifth and sixth graders, he invented a cross-cultural simulation unit that built group solidarity while teaching the rudiments of anthropology. Although this was done in school it would be entirely suitable for a Saturday Club. He divided the group into three mythical tribal cultures which he named the Mamazons, the Vorichis, and the Urbanians. The children first discussed the component strands all societies have, such as economy, religion, physical environment, technology, and social controls. Then each tribe was told about its own particulars and asked to find ways to chart them. They were asked not to divulge any specific facts about their tribe but to represent them through making artifacts, painting murals, and making dioramas of tribal custom. Each tribe then tried to discover as much as possible about the priorities, prohibitions, and problems of the other two cultures through inference and deduction. More details, and a sample myth and spiritual ritual for each culture is included in the appendix along with the name and address of the originator of the game.

In addition to readily available games such as *Risk*, a world conquest game for two to six players ages ten to adult (Parker Bros.) and *Land Grab* for two to four players ages nine to adult (House of Games, Inc., Elk Grove Village, Chicago, Illinois 60607), the 3M Co. markets the simulation games *Sleuth, Acquire, Stocks and Bonds,* and *Venture*, among others. Similies 11 in LaJolla, California 92037, offers *Explorers I, Explorers II,* and *Roaring Camp*. They will send brochures upon request. There are many others to be sure, but these will give the interested reader a place to begin.

6. *Crafts.* The extent of a craft program depends on available facilities and teachers. If there is elaborate equipment, by all means find out how to use it. If there is a teacher or a mentor with a special skill to teach, build the program around it, or at least incorporate it. If you need help getting started, there are two sources of craft projects for groups which I like. In planning for younger children,

132

roughly up to ten or eleven, consult Scholastic Funcraft Books. They offer such titles as *Magnets and Batteries, Flying Models, Paper Fun, Print and Paint, Action Toys and Action Games*. The books are colorful, the directions are clear, and the topics are appealing. For older children, roughly from ten on up, Dover Publications offers a beautifully varied selection of how-to books covering over fifty topics from dolls and dollmaking to boomerangs. They will send a catalogue on request and there is a catalogue reprint in the backs of their hardcover books. Their address is listed in the appendix.

7. *Music and drama.* Playing music in an ensemble or an orchestra offers social, intellectual, and aesthetic nourishment. If a conductor is available and there are enough skilled performers to make up a group, those blessed with musical gifts can exercise them for their own pleasure as well as the delight of those for whom they play. Depending on the size of a school, a Saturday Club, or a community, such opportunities may abound or be scarce. In a situation which appears to offer scant opportunities there may be chances for gifted children to play with adults. See the final section of this chapter for specifics.

Dramatics provides superb opportunity for imaginative interpretation, cooperation, and use of a wide variety of skills. There are chances for

acting, singing, and dancing
producing and directing
costuming and lighting
designing and building sets
advertising and ticket selling
knowing the dramatic literature and choosing appropriate plays.

Not only is a wide range of skills necessary but each member of the group depends on the others.

"To be or not to be" is merely a famous phrase until it is part of

133

that living whole called a play. When Hamlet has a costume, a stage, lighting, a set, an audience, and other characters around him, his story comes to life. No matter how talented the star, he cannot do it alone. A gifted child needs the experience of being a supporting member of the cast as well as the star.

If opportunities for children's theater do not exist locally, a Saturday Club may wish to provide them. Imagination, energy, one willing director, and a group of children are all that's needed to begin. Start with a small project, and depend on the children to write a script, help with costumes and sets, and make sound effects. Don't feel that each production must be elaborate. One group of twenty imaginative children ages nine and ten with a small budget limited their costumes to tights, turtlenecks, and masks or tunics made from paper bags. They wrote and produced a highly entertaining play about dragons. Rather than preventing expression, the lack of funds for such things as costumes was simply a spur to originality and the challenge of solving a problem.

The World of Travel

Going to a new place is an experience that unites those who share it. Because geographical location, choice of emphasis, budget, and age and number of participants differ in each case I am simply going to list several resources and references for each of four different kinds of travel.

TRAVEL/STUDYING

Many colleges offer alumni weekends or summer sessions for whole families. Room and board are included in the fee. There is a variety of course offerings, athletic and social opportunities are available, and baby-sitting can be arranged if necessary. Different

134

members of the family learn different things and can share their discoveries. For details, consult your own college, or a college or university in the part of the country you would like to visit.

Frequently, museums sponsor special-purpose trips. Some are short, some extensive, but they provide an opportunity to combine an excursion with learning. For information call a nearby museum or write one of the large ones anywhere in the country. The Museum of Natural History in New York City sponsors trips of varying duration and distance. Although some are expensive, they are very well planned.

For a resource book on this subject try *Learning Vacations* by Gerston G. Eisenberg, Acropolis Books. Of course be sure to make a thorough check on any suggestions before setting out.

TRAVEL/CAMPING

Nature is a great teacher and a great leveler. Camping offers the gifted child challenge and companionship. The Sierra Club offers local day hikes and more extended trips for groups at every age and level of experience. They also schedule work trips, which provide an opportunity to contribute to a worthwhile cause while enjoying well-planned camping and beautiful countryside at relatively small cost. Their bulletin has specific details. A hint: bus travel is a relatively inexpensive way to cover large distances with no penalty for stopovers or side trips.

National Outdoor Leadership School in Lander, Wyoming, Outward Bound, whose headquarters are in Andover, Mass., and the American Field Service, with offices all over the country, offer many trips in which members of the group must rely on one another for comfort and safety, and sometimes for survival. These are planned for participants in specific age groups, rarely below the age of fourteen.

There are camps to which whole families go together to share

135

the experience of using an axe, building a fire, climbing or pad-
dling to a destination, relying on one another, and enjoying success and songs around the campfire at the end of the day. Some
camps cater only to families and others offer family sessions which
precede or follow the camp's regular season. A local YMCA is
generally a good source of current information.

If these outings require too much equipment, are too expensive,
or too difficult to arrange, a simple day hike can serve many of the
same purposes. The point of view matters more than the number
of miles covered. An excellent resource book for city and country
families who want help planning for young children's summer
vacations is *The Sierra Club Summer Book* by Linda Allison (Sierra
Club Books, 1050 Mills Tower, San Francisco, Ca. 94104). The
fourteen parts cover such topics as Crafts, Games, and The City
Naturalist.

TRAVEL/WORKING

For those who are too young to be able to get paying jobs, there
are still opportunities to travel to a new place to serve as a volunteer.

These offer a gifted child an opportunity to solve problems,
work on programs, and give of himself. In addition to the Sierra
Club work trips mentioned earlier, another example is the Quebec
Labrador Mission, formerly known as the Grenfell Mission.
Under its auspices young men and women from the age of sixteen
up are placed in homes in Labrador where they develop and work
on community projects for a six- or eight-week period in the
summer. For further information contact the main headquarters in
Boston (Quebec Labrador Foundation, Mill Rd., Ipswich, Mass.
01938).

For information about other similar opportunities consult
American Friends Service Committee. They have offices through-

out the country. Their address in New York City is 15 Rutherford Place, New York, N.Y. 10003.

TRAVEL/SEEING A FOREIGN COUNTRY

The gifted child who would like to immerse himself in the living and language of a foreign country should contact the Experiment for International Living in Putney, Vt. 05346. They run programs themselves and know about other existing opportunities.

The reader who wishes to plan a trip in any of the four categories has a resource to consult. This is not intended to be a comprehensive list—that would be a book in itself—but rather to provide a place to begin.

Access to the Adult World

Traditional programs exist and original opportunities can be arranged through a combination of selection, stubbornness, and stamina. A good resource book to stimulate this kind of thinking is *What Color Is Your Parachute* by Richard Bolles (Ten Speed Press, Box 7123, Berkeley, Ca. 94707). Although it was written for an adult audience, many of the points it makes are applicable to a young person interested in doing something out of the ordinary.

Here are some traditional ways a gifted child can join with adults in a group endeavor.

PROGRAMS DESIGNED TO TEACH A SPECIFIC SKILL

A major city's museum education program may offer a course on restoration of furniture or paintings, a craft guild might offer a series of lessons on weaving or decoupage, or a library might offer bookbinding. An interested applicant is usually eligible if he can

137

pay the fee; admission is not decided by age or formal academic degree. If you have a museum, science center, or facility devoted to historical preservation near you, call to see what adult education programs are currently offered and whether they would accept a young applicant. We will consider college courses in the final section of this chapter. While it is difficult to arrange access to them, it is not impossible. Few things are.

VOLUNTEER SERVICE

Every community has needs to be met by those who will volunteer. This is true of individuals and groups. Such activity can be deeply satisfying to a gifted child who would like to give care as well as receive it. The same is true for a group of gifted children working together to meet a need or solve a problem. As a group can build identity through being against other groups or ideas, it can also build it through allegiance to a project or community. For specific details of local needs consult your local Voluntary Association, whose address can generally be found in the telephone book or by writing to the National Center for Voluntary Action, 1215 16th Street, N.W., Washington, D.C. 20036. This is a clearing house for volunteer programs throughout the country.

TEACHING AND TUTORING

Through day-care centers, summer camps, community programs, after-school projects, and children's hospitals there are chances for gifted children to teach or tutor other children. Examples range from a group of fifth, sixth, and seventh graders who worked in a summer remedial reading program, to seventh and eighth grade boys who taught soccer two afternoons a week after school, to Lucia, who financed a winter's worth of theater tickets by giving music lessons when she was fourteen. Just as learning how to be a member of a group is important for a gifted child, learning how to be an effective leader can be a lesson in human nature. Write to the director of whatever local facility appeals to you, or consult a volunteer association.

MUSIC AND DRAMA

The gifted young artist who wants to be part of a musical group without paying the high tuition of formal music schooling can find opportunities through churches, community groups, and those music stores that also arrange music lessons.

Churches usually welcome choir singers and are delighted to have guest instrumentalists. In addition, choir directors are often knowledgeable about choral groups who sing secular music. Frequently there is an overlap in membership of such groups and they may well share the same director.

Information about community orchestras, fife and drum corps, bands, and ensembles can be found through the community newspaper or music store. One such store, which is not unique in its approach, sells instruments, scores, and sheet music. They also sponsor and house a small music school whose faculty is made up of local musicians who are available to give lessons. The store and the music school share a large bulletin board where notices are posted of groups needing a member to play a particular instrument, or individual artists who want to join a group. Young participants are welcome in all the above. Talent is the ticket.

Opportunities for gifted children to gain access to adult theater are difficult but not impossible to arrange, particularly if the young person is willing to do backstage work. Consult a local paper for information about neighborhood amateur groups and apprentice programs for high school and college students. In such a program apprentices work side by side with professionals and though the hours are long, the learning opportunities and the

139

camaraderie are enormous. Many summer theaters offer such programs. Some are more formalized than others. If you are interested, choose several theaters on the basis of their location, their leadership, or the type of play they produce. Get in touch with them. If they do not have programs or opportunities themselves, they may be able to make some suggestions.

NONTRADITIONAL OPPORTUNITIES

Apprenticeship. Some businesses are willing to offer apprenticeships. When these are available they provide unique opportunities to learn and apply newly learned skills. These seem particularly difficult to arrange for children under the age of sixteen who do not yet have working papers, but it can be done. The key word is volunteer. Interest, coupled with the willingness to contribute time without asking for money, will open many doors. Here are four examples of young people aged thirteen, fifteen, seventeen, and nineteen who found unusual opportunities through volunteering.

When Lucia was thirteen, the summer vacation loomed long. She had been to summer camp for two years and did not wish to go again. She cared little for country club athletics and was eager to find an interesting project. She wanted to be a teacher or a camp counselor but it was hard for her to establish her credibility. Too young for the payroll, she volunteered at a day camp for handicapped children. The first few days she was only allowed to tie shoelaces and serve snacks, but then she found a way to start helping in the swimming pool and put on puppet shows. As the children responded to her and she proved herself reliable, the staff came to trust her and genuinely appreciated the imagination she brought to the program. Before two weeks were over she was fully accepted. She was not paid in money, but she earned respect, a place on an adult team, and she received an opportunity to be a giver of care.

Chris, at fifteen, was fascinated by botany and too young for working papers. By volunteering, he wangled his way into an organization that combined a commercial nursery with a research program. At that time the researchers were working to develop a strain of flowering shrub that would be highly resistant to automobile exhaust. Starting with a broom in the laboratory, Chris made himself useful and by the end of his ten-week stay he had a white coat and a name plate. His colleagues seemed to have forgotten he didn't share their extensive training, age, or tax bracket. He was quick to learn, reliable, and interested and those qualities earned him his place on the team.

Susan, highly intellectual and seventeen, ached for a summer opportunity in the New York City publishing world. Jobs were scarce and her chances seemed slim indeed but she was determined. She concentrated on five places she admired and, through diligent searching and help from her family, she found a connection with an editor at one of the five. She wrote him a letter explaining her interest, saying why she had chosen his firm, listing her credentials, describing what she thought she could offer, and saying she would be delighted to work for the experience—she was not asking for a salary. She concluded her articulate letter by volunteering to work in the files. According to the editor, that did it. Today he says, "Anybody who goes to the trouble of finding out that much about your company . . . who likes it that much . . . who has done that much research and is willing to work for no pay has to get a break . . . and after a couple of weeks of watching the files get cleaned out I got a guilty conscience, so I gave her something fun." Susan has had increasingly interesting work given her summer after summer, finally accompanied by a paycheck. She will graduate from college next June with knowledge, training,

141

practical experience, and excellent references from four summers' worth of work.

One young man spent the summer of 1978 as an assistant to a geology professor who is mapping an interior region of a foreign country. The student traveled at his own expense. He could afford it and thought that the opportunity to work side by side with a man whose work he admires was a worthwhile investment in his own future—the equivalent of taking a private course. Those who can afford to volunteer for such positions and would like to do so should put up a notice on a departmental bulletin board of a college or university, or write a letter to the chairman of the department, whose name can be found in the college catalogue.

Not every apprenticeship will or should lead to a permanent career in the same field. That is not their value for the gifted child. Their importance lies in the opportunity they present for a young person of drive and ability to learn new skills and practice them professionally. When looking for similar opportunities keep in mind the three suggestions at the end of this chapter.

Advanced study. To arrange for a gifted child to take advanced courses you again need a combination of selection, stubbornness, and stamina. Most colleges, even those offering extension programs, will not admit students under the age of eighteen or those who do not have a high school diploma or its equivalent. Even though the student may have the prerequisite knowledge, his family is willing and able to pay the tuition, and he is not seeking transferable academic credit, formal college policy usually denies him admission. The head of the continuing education department in a medium-sized private liberal arts college in New England had this advice for anyone who wants to enroll an unusual student: "If the admissions office says no, don't give up. Try the continuing education office, the office of nondegree programs or its equivalent. Try to see the head of one of those offices in person. Know exactly what course or courses you are interested in, what they

142

will cover and what the prerequisites are. You will help your own cause by being well-informed. A college official will be able to plead your cause for you more effectively if you have done your homework. If all the officials say no, go directly to the department head, or the professor who teaches the course. Don't give up!"

Arranging for a gifted child to have access to the adult world is not easy but three things help:

1. Decide on a field.
2. Find a specific person.
3. Volunteer!

Summary

Children's programs, travel, and access to the adult world offer enrichment that need not be solitary. These group activities are appropriate for children who are gifted, children who are quick, or children who are interested.

In writing this chapter I faced a choice—should I speak in generalizations and thus risk superficiality, or should I speak in specifics and risk both omission and giving information that may go out of date? Having chosen the latter, I gave considerable space to ideas and activities I have not seen described in other books or catalogues and simply mentioned by name those that are more in the realm of common knowledge. Consequently, the space devoted to various descriptions is not indicative of their relative importance.

Each combination of people, location, need, and inclination will be different. As the choices are being made, let the children themselves be active agents, not passive recipients. The result will be enthusiasm, excitement, and commitment.

Chapter 8

Stories

Reading aloud to a child is an ideal way to help him enrich his internal language, and this automatically increases his supply of expressive tools. Language is contagious.

Gifted children use receptive and expressive language to manage some of their most powerful intellectual and emotional hungers. The child who is comfortable with words will play with them, will collect them as treasures, and because he can listen to them and comprehend them, he will be able to use them to express his ideas and feelings. The child thus builds a platform of language from which to launch rockets of abstract thinking and is free to venture, risk, learn, and create.

Since you cannot express what you do not have, the gifted child first needs a well-developed, receptive language facility. People, like television sets, are receivers as well as transmitters. Many images and sounds come in from the air. The viewer chooses what appeals to him after consulting the program guide, or by flicking from channel to channel to see what's there. Once the choice is made, the channel receives and transmits only one program at a time. While others still exist in the air, they are not tuned in, so they are not a distraction. The gifted child who absorbs so much, yet struggles to experience the world with inadequate language, is like a television set with all channels receiving simultaneously, no station selector, and no controls for horizontal hold, brightness, and hue.

A child needs to change fantasy from something which controls him to something which he controls in order to grow up. Language bridges fact and fiction. The greater the texture and variety of the gifted child's vocabulary, the more he can master his rich imaginings. Many gifted children automatically apply language to this task but others need help or extra exposure to words.

The gifted child whose personal lexicon is filled with words of texture and strength has many ways of expressing his own thoughts, many of which may be difficult to articulate because they are so original. He also develops many ways to meet the writer when he is reading something new. Real reading is active and energetic. The reader matches an expectation in his head with what his eyes find as they travel along a line of print. Katrina de Hirsch refers to this as "casting a linguistic shadow." With it the reader anticipates what is to come and easily appreciates cadence, rhythm, and humor. The gifted child who is familiar with pattern and theme and is accustomed to hearing the various languages of fairy tales, humor, suspense, journalism, poetry, and commercials, to name but a few, will read these languages with ease and accuracy, distinguishing them from one another.

In addition to enhancing language, reading aloud has at least five other benefits we should consider. These are important to all children, but they are vital nourishment for the gifted child.

1. Expansion of knowledge.
2. Exercise of imagination.

146

3. Identification with character and the opportunity to share feelings and experiences far beyond his own with a family group or a class.
4. Bibliotherapy, the comfort of finding one's own dilemma described or resolved in stories.
5. Experience of intellectual pleasure and the physical and emotional closeness of sharing a lap or a sofa as well as a story.

Some surprising fears and foibles explain why more adults don't read aloud. The first is a fear that in some way it is "spoiling" the child to read to him once he starts to read by himself. "Shouldn't he be reading to me?" a parent will say. "After all, he's learning to read in school. Shouldn't he practice at home?" Yes, if he wants, but that is no substitute for being read to. We must separate mastery of decoding from enrichment and linguistic pleasure. These are two sides of the language coin. A child can understand things read to him years before he can read them independently, and long before they can read by themselves children love to tell stories. For little children, particularly those with a gift for language, get some books without words. Mercer Mayer has assembled some excellent ones. Among them are *The Great Cat Chase* (Scholastic), *A Boy, a Dog, a Frog and a Friend,* and *Hiccup* (Dial Press) and *Two Moral Tales: Bear's New Clothes and Bird's New Hat* and *Two More Moral Tales: Just a Pig at Heart and Sly Fox's Folly* (Four Winds Press). The illustrations in all of them leave no doubt about the story line but the child tells it in his own words.

Some parents avoid reading aloud because they aren't sure how to pick "the right book." Flanked by this is a horror that, if they once begin, they'll be trapped into reading something boring or demeaning. Some books written for youthful ears are of such thin literary quality that it is humiliating for an intelligent adult to read them aloud. The child detects the distaste immediately, and lacking in experience, attributes it to the activity, not the literary selection. The noble sacrifice is useless and the child is disappointed.

Here's a different way of approaching the problem which may banish the fears and foibles. Let the adult find his or her own favorite kind of story, written on a level appropriate for young listeners.

If you, as an adult, enjoy Jane Austen, read the *Frances* books by Russell Hoban (Harper and Row) to a child. They are filled with parallel puckish profundity, and a tartly accurate view of human relations and social custom. Frances and her little sister Gloria are reminiscent of the Bennett sisters in *Pride and Prejudice*, and the language is delicious!

Are you comedy-of-manners-and-morals freak? Try *Goops*, and Hilaire Belloc's *Cautionary Verses* on your way to the *Importance of Being Earnest*.

Do you thrill to The Forces of Nature Harnessed and Unharnessed? Try *The Wreck of the Hesperus* and Jack London on the way to Admiral Byrd's *Discovery* and *Alone*, or Charles Lindbergh's *The Spirit of St. Louis*.

If you believe the child is the embodiment of truth and healing and, as an adult, love *Silas Marner*, read *The Emperor's New Clothes*, or Menotti's *Amahl and the Night Visitors* to children.

I once heard a concert of brasses in which the musicians talked about melody and various musical forms: waltzes, marches, scherzos. Then they played *Jingle Bells* in each one. You should hear it as a chorale—it brings tears to the eyes! We, adults and children together, learned to discover the pattern as well as recognize the melody. The same thing can be done with literature.

As linguistic foreshadowing is prerequisite to real reading, so familiarity with a literary theme adds extra dimension to enjoyment of the printed word. Entertaining and important literary themes appear in well-written children's books, as well as in the classics and books written for the adult popular market. Great

148

dreams and stories are found in slender volumes as well as in thick ones. A book is not a sirloin steak that must be two inches thick to merit adult attention or satisfy an adult appetite.

Let's choose five patterns and see on how many levels they appear.

Pattern 1: Psychological Forces at Work in the Community

Pity, greed, passion, sacrifice, love, and death. For a young child? Yes. In this exercise, I'll say that *War and Peace, Gone with the Wind, Middlemarch,* and *Charlotte's Web* are all the same story. They come in different depths and on different levels, to be sure, but they are still the same story. The first three (the so-called adult ones) are laced with social and political history. All kinds of people and many kinds of values are represented. Economics collides with idealism against an agrarian backdrop. The same is true of the fourth!

Try to return these two quotes to their rightful covers.

Although he loved her children and her grandchildren, none of the new ones ever quite took her place in his heart. She was in a class by herself. It is not often that someone comes along who is a true friend and a good writer. _____was both.[1]

For the growing good of the world is partly dependent on unhistoric acts; and that things are not so ill with you and me as they might have been, is half owing to the number who have lived faithfully a hidden life and rest in unvisited tombs.[2]

[1]E. B. White, *Charlotte's Web* (New York: Harper & Row, 1952), p. 184.
[2]George Eliot, *Middlemarch* (Boston: Houghton Mifflin Co., Riverside Edition, 1956), p. 613.

149

WHAT ELSE THEY NEED

Is this a table of contents for a saga of Russian life, people playing out their lives in the English countryside, or a story of a pig and a spider?

Although in *Charlotte's Web* some of the characters are animals, they act the way people act, and have a human balance of good and bad qualities apiece. Even Templeton, the rat, has moments when the noblest among us must identify with him.

Fern and her father collide early in the story. Mr. Arable is a knowledgeable farmer, well-meaning father, keeper of the Ten Commandments, and also family provider. But he appears to his daughter as a cruel supporter of a double standard. Her vision has

[3]White, Table of Contents.

150

not yet been clouded by worldly compromise between money and morality. Their disagreement involves a choice between practicality and compassion. Should Wilbur be killed? Which should win? What of the leader who makes the cold-blooded choice? How would you feel about him as a father, as a husband, as a town councilor, a tax collector, a minister, or perhaps a doctor? If he were your physician, would you dare to get sick? The arguments on each side are familiar to readers of New Testament parables, Sinclair Lewis, and the Watergate tapes, as well as the four books under discussion.

Charlotte is the practical achiever, as are the team of Arable and Zuckerman. Both are loving, both are sure of right as they see it, but they are on opposite sides. Who will win and how can the author apportion victory without defeating virtue?

In the case of *Charlotte's Web,* the device is just the same as it is in the other stories. By shifting the focus to a newly developing trait in a familiar character, the author changes the balance of the story and a new tack is permissible. Enter love!—a new kind. I'm not going to try to pretend I find Henry Fussy as romantic as Rhett Butler—but don't tell Fern!

England, Russia, and the Old South know the men of affairs whose efforts succeed. So does E. B. White.

A great feeling of happiness swept over the Zuckermans and the Arables. This was the greatest moment in Mr. Zuckerman's life. It is deeply satisfying to win a prize in front of a lot of people.[4]

These 184 pages bring forth tears, laughter, suspense, and transportation into another world. "Salutations," as Charlotte herself might say to all writers who are "humble," "versatile," and "radiant."

One might imagine George Eliot, E. B. White, Margaret

[4]Ibid., p. 160.

151

Mitchell, or Tolstoy saying of their artistic aim, "It is not to resolve a question irrefutably, but to compel one to love life in all its manifestations—and these are inexhaustible."

Which one said:

> If I were told that I could write a novel in which I could indisputably establish as true my point of view on all social questions, I would not dedicate two hours to such a work; but if I were told that what I wrote would be read twenty years from now by those who are children today, and that they would weep and laugh over it, and fall in love with the life in it, then I would dedicate all my existence and all my power to it.[5]

I am not advocating that *Charlotte's Web* take the place of *War and Peace,* or either of the other two books, but I am suggesting that the adult who enjoys one will enjoy the others, and the child who is introduced to this kind of book by way of a book like *Charlotte's Web* will find the territory hospitable and familiar, and hence will probably journey there independently in later years.

Here are some books which I have enjoyed reading aloud and which the children to whom I have read them remember vividly. The age suggestions were appropriate to my circumstances but there is nothing sacred about them.

Ages 4–8
   Bedtime for Frances, etc.   Russell Hoban
   A Holiday for Edith and the Bears, etc.   Dare Wright

Ages 8 and up
   Charlie and the Chocolate Factory   Roald Dahl
   Charlotte's Web   E. B. White
   Stuart Little   E. B. White
   A Christmas Carol   Charles Dickens

---

[5]Leo Tolstoy, *War and Peace,* trans. Rosemary Edmonds (London: Penguin Books Ltd., Society Edition, 1971), p. 10.

The Wind in the Willows   Kenneth Grahame
The Lonely Doll Learns a Lesson, etc.   Dare Wright
The Fairy Doll   Rumer Godden
Norse Gods and Giants   Ingri and Edgar d'Aulaire

Ages 10 and up
Danny, Champion of the World   Roald Dahl
Living Free   Joy Adamson
Little Women   Louisa May Alcott
The Doll's House   Rumer Godden
The Snow Goose   Paul Gallico
The Yearling   Marjorie K. Rawlings
Anne and the Sand Dobbies   John Coburn

Judy Blume writes excellent books for the independent reader. Two specific titles are *Are You There God, It's Me, Margaret* and *Tales of a Fourth Grade Nothing.* Children find these both personal and satisfying to read alone, so I would not recommend reading them aloud. Some adults who admired her earlier books strongly disapprove of the sexual content of *Forever.* Follow your personal preference in encouraging or discouraging a child to read it.

An imaginative, humorous, and beautifully written book for readers of all ages is *The Pluperfect of Love* by Dorothy Crayder.

Pattern 2: Human Nature, Good or Evil?

Children and, incidentally, philosophers have wondered about this forever. Is human nature gentle and benevolent, to be encouraged and set free? Is it dangerous, something which must be contained by powerful bonds? The gifted child, whose perception of discrepancy is so acute, may be relieved to discover that this question has troubled wise authors throughout the ages.

The mark of a mature mind is the ability to hold two opposing ideas at once, which is to say to be comfortable with ambiguity. Don't expect this of most children below the age of eleven or twelve, which, as we know from Piaget, is the age when abstract thinking develops as part of formal operations. For children younger than this, the simple process of sorting good from bad is fun, and lays good foundations for later, more complicated thinking. Adults who treasure *The Turn of the Screw, Lord of the Flies, Billy Budd,* and *Song of Myself* may be surprised that there are counterparts in books which theoretically belong to children.

Begin with *The Bad Island* by William Steig. For majestic language it's hard to match. There are huge rumbling words children love to hear long before they can pronounce them or use them independently.

The Start of the Battle

Eventually things really got out of hand, or out of claw and talon. From blaming, and cursing and insulting, and threatening and insulting and hitting, they went on to serious fighting. And all their deepest demons of hate broke loose. Much as they had all loathed and abominated one another before, it was nothing compared to the way they loathed and abominated now. But loathing and abominating no longer gave them enjoyment.[6]

The Battle

It went on and on and on and one day it was finally over. Everyone had succeeded in killing everyone else off. The last ugly ogre had given his last ugly gasp and the last serpent breathed its last flame and the island was a gigantic heap of dead, scaly, thorny, fanged, horned, bug-eyed, barbed, bristling, saw-toothed carcasses, lying in ashes and embers, burning and giving off a dark, horrible smoke. And then there was nothing but hot ashes.[7]

[6] William Steig, *The Bad Island* (New York: Simon & Schuster, Windmill Books, 1969), unpaged.
[7] Ibid.

The denouement belongs to Steig and his readers, but there is no ambiguity. His good is as good as his evil is evil. And no, the children won't be scared. You might progress from there to sorting good children from bad children. *A Child's Garden of Verses* works for this, as do *Cautionary Tales, The Bad Child's Book of Beasts, More Beasts for Worse Children,* and *A Moral Alphabet* by Hilaire Belloc, and *The Goop Books* by Gelett Burgess. A child who would otherwise feel too old to be reading "baby-stuff" will enjoy reading children's poetry searching for adult distinctions. And all children will feel a warm rush of superiority reading about other children who are totally bad.

Here are some books from which young gifted listeners have drawn enjoyment and thoughtful perceptions.

Ages 4 and up
Two books of photographs:
The Family of Man   Edward Steichen
Family   Margaret Mead and Ken Heyman
The Bad Island   William Steig
Lucy McLockett   Phyllis McGinley

Ages 8 and up
Pinocchio   Carlo Coloddi
Trolls   Ingri and Edgar d'Aulaire
Nora's Tale   Edith Vonnegut Rivera
Fables   Aesop
A Child's Garden of Verses   Robert Louis Stevenson
Poems Every Child Should Know   Eugene Field
Goops and How to Be Them   Gelett W. Burgess
Goops and How Not To Be Them   Gelett W. Burgess
Cautionary Verses   Hilaire Belloc
Manners Can Be Fun   Munro Leaf

155

WHAT ELSE THEY NEED

Ages 10 and up
  Miracle in the Wilderness   Paul Gallico
  The Call of the Wild   Jack London
  The Velveteen Rabbit   Margery Williams
  The Little Mermaid   Hans Christian Andersen
  Julie of the Wolves   Jean George

Pattern 3: Time and Space: Science Fiction

We count on time and space to give shape to our lives. They make boundaries which we interpret as safety. Some people are uncomfortable when these concepts are bent or distorted, which may explain why we have made a separate category for such stories: science fiction. It's as though this gives us a safe way to play with potentially dangerous ideas. For adults who are devotees of Jules Verne or Isaac Asimov here are some suggested stories for gifted children.

The story of *Peter Pan* can be both soothing and liberating to a gifted child who may feel like a Ping-Pong ball traveling between paddles of omnipotence and dependence. Personally, I find a story version more manageable than trying to read the actual play aloud.

With reality in one hand, hold Ann Lindbergh's volume of poems, *The Unicorn,* in the other. Read the section on Sky and the Winds of Time. Who better to lead you through the stars, and give a whole new dimension to your reality than this explorer-poet? Once you have stepped into this amplified world, the list of people with more secrets to tell is endless. Miraculously, their stories are for all ages. Here are a few specific suggestions from an enormous number of possibilities: *The Little Prince* by Antoine de Saint-Exupéry, *A Wrinkle in Time* by Madeleine L'Engle, *The Wonderful Adventures of Nils* by Selma Lagerlof, and *The Phantom Tollbooth* by Norton Juster.

Special mention must be made of *The Lion, The Witch and The Wardrobe,* the first book in the series *The Chronicles of Narnia* by the British philosopher and theologian C. S. Lewis. Through an entertaining, seemingly simple story, this book makes profound observations on time, space, and human nature.

Books by Ray Bradbury are popular with old and young enthusiasts alike. Science fiction stories do not separate into age categories in the same way other types of narratives do. But a word of caution: save *Alice in Wonderland* for much older children. An adolescent meeting it for the first time has had an appropriate treat preserved for an appropriate time.

Pattern 4: Hero Stories

Hero stories frequently have powerful appeal for a gifted child. A story of dream and conquest can match wishes he may be unable to articulate. The wishes may be ones he cannot or dare not put into words and the dreams may be so grandiose he would fear mockery if they were known.

If you, as an adult, love reading *Sailing Alone Around the World, The Odyssey, Jason and the Golden Fleece,* and other myths and fairy tales, read Maurice Sendak's thirty-seven-page picture book, *Where the Wild Things Are,* to a gifted child. Sendak and Homer? Yes. To see how beautifully they fit together, first remember the components of a traditional hero story and then look at Sendak's plot. The fact jumps out that each has the ingredients and story line of a classic hero tale: the task, the journey, the confrontation, and the return. The task is defined in terms of obstacles that are frequently ferocious, uncontrolled or uncontrollable beasts which must be outwitted or tamed as Theseus vanquished the Minotaur and Odysseus tricked the Cyclops. Both of these are classical heroes. Psychoanalysis introduced us to the story of man trying to

157

tame himself, a tricky adversary, as we know from *Equus* or *I Never Promised You a Rose Garden,* and the modern hero's task is to vanquish alienation.

The journey takes the hero away from familiar surroundings, out of sight of those who might protect or help him, into a different country where the language and customs are probably unfamiliar. Although he may travel through a deep forest or through the air, the main journey is frequently over water. Water symbolizes many different things and represents comfort and danger simultaneously.

Next comes a confrontation, with a cunning, powerful, or seductive adversary. Usually something tempts the hero to join the opposition and to abandon his quest, but then he finds a way to resist and return home, having accomplished his deed. The passing of time will usually have been marked by the changing of seasons, or, if it is a story in a dream, day will have changed to night and back again within the dream, regardless of externals. This is the storyteller's device for indicating the making and closing of a circle. We meet the hero, learn his charge, see him off, and wait for his return, knowing he will be beyond our sight—on the dark side of the moon—until his reappearance.

Odysseus and Jason each make circular journeys and so, in *Where the Wild Things Are,* does Max, whose task is to tame himself —the first three pages leave no doubt about that. Then swiftly comes the setting for the voyage, complete with forest, ocean, and boat. No picture of Jason in the *Argo* could show more lust for adventure and pride in captaincy than does the picture of Max as he sets out to sail "through night and day, and in and out of weeks and almost over a year to where the wild things are." First he tamed them. Then he joined them with his glorious hymn to bacchanalia. "And now," cried Max, "let the wild rumpus start!" Seduction reigns. Medea, Circe, and the Sirens, as rendered by Sendak, are irresistible. The quest is abandoned—but not for good. Homesickness and the need for tempered love claim our hero and he turns his back on the wild things. He acknowledges them, but they cannot devour him, even though they threaten to. He is able to turn his back on them and wave goodbye. He is ready for the return. The ocean is ready, so is his boat, and he returns to his familiar surroundings—mission accomplished. The language in this story is a beautiful blend of realistic and fanciful, and the artwork is superb. It is a favorite among all the children I know. In psychological terms, it describes a journey all children—and all grown-ups—make repeatedly.

Are there only male heroes and voyagers? No, indeed. Listen to Phyllis McGinley.

Girl's Eye View of Relatives
The thing to remember about fathers is, they're men.
A girl has to keep it in mind.
They are dragon-seekers, bent on improbable rescues.
Scratch any father, and you find
Someone chock full of qualms and romantic terrors,
Believing change is a threat—
Like your first shoes with heels on, like your first bicycle
It took such months to get.

Walk in strange woods, they warn you about the snakes there.
Climb and they fear you'll fall.
Books, angular boys or swimming in deep water—
Fathers mistrust them all.
Men are worriers. It is difficult for them
To learn what they must learn:
How you have a journey to take and very likely,
For a while, will not return.[8]

[8]Phyllis McGinley, *Times Three* (New York, The Viking Press, 1960), p. 42.

WHAT ELSE THEY NEED

Here are a few other suggestions which are personal favorites of mine and the children to whom I have read them.

Ages 4 and up
  Where the Wild Things Are   Maurice Sendak

Ages 8 and up
  Greek Myths   Ingri and Edgar d'Aulaire
  James and the Giant Peach   Roald Dahl
  Lona, a Fairy Tale   Dare Wright

Ages 10 and up
  King Arthur and the Knights of the Round Table   Golden
    Illustrated Classic
  The Boy Who Sailed Around the World   Robin Graham
  White Fang   Jack London
  Kon Tiki   Thor Heyerdahl

Pattern 5: Magic and Wish Fulfillment

Gifted children need fantasies of power in order to feel some sense of control in their lives. If they can be strong and big, they can lead their lives by decision, not by default. If they are always small, while their parents (and siblings) and the world are always big, they cannot. Passivity is the product of ineffectiveness, and of course this perpetuates itself. However, growing up is an aggressive activity. All children need to be able to try on the mantle of power without being mocked. This kind of story provides opportunities for pretending without risk of guilt.

With guilt out the window, and fantasy permissible, consider the glory of such wish-fulfillment–dream-come-true stories as *Jane Eyre*. The frail young governess, poor but noble, meets the person and the life she wants. Just when everything seems within her grasp, it is snatched away by cruel intervening forces. What

160

happens, subsequently, to those forces? One by one they die or are removed to dreadful ends. How delicious! For little girls there can be no more satisfying example of a wish-fulfillment story than *A Little Princess*. Sara Crewe is by turns rich and kind, impoverished and noble, and rescued and forgiving—but dreadful fates befall those who were cruel to her along the way. Shudder to consider the final days of Miss Minchin.

It is important to distinguish between wish-fulfillment stories with happy endings and those with tragic endings, which is to say, the difference between fairy tales and myths. Fairy tales have happy endings. Myths have tragic endings because they usually describe human attempts to usurp godly powers, which must, of course, be punished. This is the difference between Cinderella and King Midas and why Sara Crewe can be set free and Icarus must fall.

It is a comfortable step from *Huckleberry Finn*, the adult book, to the child's book, *How Tom Fooled Captain Najork and His Hired Sportsmen* by Russell Hoban. A part of every one of us is set free each time Tom, surely a gifted child and a quintessential divergent thinker, outwits Aunt Fidget Wonkham-Strong, scrupulous keeper of convergent codes and wearer of an iron hat. He scores a run for imagination and independence when, spurning his dinner of greasy bloaters, he defeats the well-rehearsed uniformed opposition in successive games of Sneed-ball, Muck, and Womble. Enjoy life, Tom, with Aunt Bundle-Joy-Cozy-Sweet, the companion you finally find. Mark Twain would applaud your success and your taste.

Some wish-fulfillment stories depend on magic and the supernatural rather than on circumstance or coincidence. Surely therein lies the appeal of that classic pair in American folklore: Clark Kent, mild-mannered reporter for a major metropolitan daily, and second, silhouetted behind him—faster than a speeding bullet, more powerful than a locomotive, able to leap tall buildings at a single bound—synthesis of dreams come true—Superman.

WHAT ELSE THEY NEED

In *Puss 'n Boots,* the seemingly worthless cat brings wealth and the hand of the Princess to his master. In *The Bad Island,* one little flower conquers all. And in *The Brave Cowboy* by Joan Walsh Anglund, the small boy wearing a cowboy hat, playing near his front door, is in fact intrepid explorer, successful hunter of vicious beasts, and champion of the right through relentless war against outlaws. The gifted child who feels surges of intellectual strength in the confines of a childish body can forestall frustration through imagining.

Here are some suggestions:

Ages 4 and up
    Behold Man   Lennart Nilsson
      a book of photographs which provide endless trompe l'oeil surprises.
    The Brave Cowboy   Joan Walsh Anglund
    And to Think That I Saw It on Mulberry St.   Dr. Seuss

Ages 8 and up
    The Story of the Bad Little Boy Who Didn't Come to Grief
    Mark Twain
    How Tom Fooled Captain Najork and His Hired Sportsmen
    Russell Hoban
    The Wizard of Oz, etc.   L. Frank Baum
    Great Swedish Fairy Tales   selected by Elsa Olenius
    The Happy Prince and Other Tales   Oscar Wilde
    Fairy Tales   Hans Christian Andersen
    Fairy Tales   Grimm
    Norse Gods and Giants   Ingri and Edgar d'Aulaire
    The Red Fairy Book   Andrew Lang
    The Blue Fairy Book   Andrew Lang
    Wishes, Lies and Dreams   Kenneth Koch
    Mary Poppins P. L. Travers

Ages 10 and up
  Mrs. 'arris Goes to Paris, etc.   Paul Gallico
  Thomasina   Paul Gallico
  The Man Who Was Magic   Paul Gallico
  A Little Princess   Frances Hodgson Burnett
  The Secret Garden   Frances Hodgson Burnett
  Harriet, the Spy   Louise Fitzhugh
  Pippi Longstocking, etc.   Astrid Lundgren
  Freaky Friday   Mary Rodgers

The patterns and titles I have mentioned are intended to be representative, not encyclopedic. You will find others you prefer or want to add. Gifted children, particularly, need to feel at home with rich vocabulary, narrative, explanations, imagery, rhythm, and metaphor. They need to absorb many different kinds of language both for pure enjoyment and as a way of increasing their own expressive capabilities.

Pick the kind of book *you* as an adult enjoy reading and find it on a level appropriate to the child, or children, you want to read to. Do not fear forcing your taste on them. Enthusiasm is contagious. You may well introduce the child to something you enjoy at a level satisfying to him. Chances are this alone will produce a lifelong convert. You are, in effect, taking him on a trip to a country always accessible to re-exploration. At the least, the child will enjoy your willingness, physical closeness, and attention as well as the words he hears. Let him catch language from you through literature.

For those who would enjoy studying this topic further, here are some books I, personally, enjoy and from which I have learned a great deal.

The Uses of Enchantment   Bruno Bettelheim
The Green and Burning Tree   Eleanor Cameron
The Hero with a Thousand Faces   Joseph Campbell

WHAT ELSE THEY NEED

The Masks of God   Joseph Campbell
Language and Myth   Ernst Cassirer
Language and the Discovery of Reality   Joseph Church
Myth and Reality   Mircea Eliade
Myths, Dreams and Mysteries   Mircea Eliade
Childhood and Society   Erik H. Erikson
The Magic Years   Selma Fraiberg
The Birth of Language   Shulamith Kastein and B. Trace
The Miracle of Language   Charlton Laird
Thought and Language   L. S. Vygotsky

PART IV

What They Say

Chapter 9

The Gifted Speak

Biographies allow us to see what well-known people have done with their lives. Some, like Alexander Calder, build success and find fulfillment and enjoyment in work well into old age Some, like Ernest Hemingway, create, struggle, and rage. Others, like John Keats or Edna St. Vincent Millay, sing a brief song of piercing beauty and die.

Looking back on a completed life is very different from predicting what course a life will take. It is impossible to say in advance which gifted people will fulfill their promise, which will dilute or scatter their treasure, or which will make outstanding contributions starting from seemingly modest beginnings.

The people in this chapter are intellectually outstanding. While they are different in talent, background, schooling, and age (they range from six to seventy-five), they are alike in seeming to be gifted. Each has dilemmas and goals, and each was asked the question, "If you had three wishes what would they be?"

167

WHAT THEY SAY

Eddie, Age 6

Eddie is six years old and has been identified as a gifted child by a California public school which honors intellectual achievement and has a new program for gifted children. He is one of three children in a bright, enterprising family. His parents say that Eddie's brothers do well in school, they are lively and quick to understand, but Eddie is different. His brothers think so too. His reading and mathematics are two or three years beyond grade level. He reads music, plays the piano, and is eager to learn a foreign language. He has an enormous store of general knowledge gathered from the media and absorbed from general conversation. Furthermore, he can play with his knowledge, extrapolate from it, and reapply it to different situations. This distinguishes him from a pseudo-gifted child who has been overtaught and simply trained to recite.

Eddie is a busy, happy child who is content to dig to China at the beach along with other six-year-old excavators. He does not have a special dilemma at the moment, but his parents do.

They waver between wanting to treat him like everyone else and wanting different things for him. They want to share their pride with the world, proclaim him gifted, yet they don't want to separate him from other children. They want to recognize his difference, but they do not want him to have to pay a social price for it. They are caught in a conflict between acknowledgment and secrecy. They must choose among acceleration, segregation, or enrichment in his schooling. If he stays in his present school, he will be moved into a program for children identified as gifted. His parents ask two questions. Is the labeling itself a healthy thing? Is the curriculum designed for expressing and training or is it merely an express train?

If his parents move Eddie to the independent school half an hour away, he will be separated from his brothers and his neighborhood friends. If he stays in a regular section of his public school, will his

168

intellectual curiosity be stimulated and satisfied by whatever extracurricular enrichment activities are available? Must there be an inevitable choice between boasting and blooming, or hiding and hurting?

Eddie's three wishes are:

to have as many more wishes as I want;
to burp louder than anyone else in the world;
to be able to fly.

Peter, Age 13

Peter has just turned thirteen. He is one of two children of professional parents, both of whom work at a high level in demanding careers. In addition, each makes a strong commitment to local and national social issues. Peter attends an academically challenging coeducational country day school outside New York City where he is the outstanding scholar of the 150 children in his division. He is a fine athlete. For many years he was a handsome, shy boy with a secret.

Starting at age eight he traveled into New York three or four afternoons a week to attend the School of American Ballet, directed by George Balanchine. He studied, practiced, and performed—telling no one outside his immediate family.

As a little child he had struggled to overcome social timidity and he had worked hard to make a place for himself among his classmates. Friendly, scrupulously fair and compassionate, with a highly developed sense of justice, he had seen other children suffer pain from ridicule or exclusion. Each community has its own customs and codes. Peter's community does not emphasize artistic enlightenment. Peter was not going to invite difficulty by admitting that he was a ballet dancer. Nor was he willing to run the risk

169

that something as pure to him as his love of dancing might be soiled by mockery.

He led a double life, dreading discovery. Each winter brought panic. The students in his ballet school make up the company which performs *The Nutcracker* at Lincoln Center. For several years he was simply one of the cast. His name was printed in tiny letters in the back of the program and he hid whenever a VIP tour came backstage in case someone from his school might be in the group.

But his gifts insisted on living, and demanded exercise. His heart was with them, although his mind required the safety of camouflage. Once again an element of hiding and hurting was an inevitable part of a gifted child's life.

Each year Peter grew bolder, as though the kind of strength he was developing in his dancer's muscles was growing, too, in his emotional and intellectual fiber. When he was eleven he confided his secret to a selected number of trusted friends. He felt strong enough to risk having to hear and answer:

"Ballet? Ballet? What are you? Some kind of a sissy?"

"Dancing's for girls."

"Dancers are queers."

He and his family knew that such remarks might come from un-enlightened people—students in his school, or their parents.

When Peter turned twelve he was cast in the leading role of the Prince. He was interviewed by CBS for the evening news; his name was in large letters in the program; he was totally visible, totally identifiable. His secret belonged to the world.

His performances were exquisite. Audiences gave themselves willingly to him as they do when they know they are safely in the hands of an artist.

170

During the run of *The Nutcracker,* Peter commuted to New York. Each day he would go to school, travel into the city, dance (sometimes two performances), receive waves of applause, return to the country, and appear the following day in school—homework done, ready to learn, maintaining academic excellence and locker room camaraderie.

At thirteen he will dance the role of the Prince again, knowing that the moment of decision is coming. He must choose whether or not dance will be his career. An affirmative decision would mean a nearly total commitment of time, physical presence, and emotional energy with no guarantee that his success will continue past the bodily changes of adolescence. Thirteen is very young to make a decision which is a gamble and which will have such a far-reaching effect. There are many family footsteps he could follow in other directions. The keenness of his intellect puts any profession within his grasp. He could aim to be a lawyer, a physicist, a philosopher, a physician—or a ballet dancer.

In the concluding scene of *The Nutcracker,* the child Prince and child Princess fly slowly into the sky in a beautiful, glistening sleigh decorated with candy—quintessential wish-fulfillment.

When Peter climbs into the sleigh and rides off into the sky for the last time will he be saying goodbye to his childhood and the dance which has been such a cherished part of it, or will he be flying into the demands and uncertainties of an artistic career?

When asked for his three wishes Peter was boyishly, appropriately fresh and said, "The first one is not to have to be in that book." Since that was not granted, he continued:

to be a principal dancer with the New York City Ballet Company and then go to college and get a good job;
to be able to stay at school for the whole day without having to leave in the middle;
to enjoy life.

171

WHAT THEY SAY

Meg, Age 20

Meg, nearly twenty, is one of four children. Her father commutes daily to New York City. Her mother is busy and happy in their exurban community. Meg attended an academically demanding country day school where her performance was adequate but not outstanding. She went on to boarding school where she was very active in such student affairs as the magazine, the glee club, and varsity athletics. She seemed the definition of "an all-around good kid." She is now doing breathtaking work in science in her sophomore year at Yale. She said, "It feels so good not to have to hide how much you know. I've always had to do that before. I always thought I had to pretend I was trying to figure things out like everybody else. Now I feel as if I'm standing in a big strong wind. It feels good."

Meg wishes:

to be able to draw and paint;
to be able to wish myself to any place in the world whenever I
    want;
to know what I want to be.

Andrew, Age 26

Andrew is one of three sons of parents who each have busy professional lives. He attended an independent school in a large northeastern city, went off to a highly competitive boarding school, Ivy League college, and business school.

He completed his education without seeming to give it much thought—prowling, effortlessly absorbing what was presented, and consistently showing an uncanny ability to solve problems. As an amusing example, although Andrew overflows with ideas,

172

he has never enjoyed putting words on paper. In order to complete ninth grade, his school required each member of the class to write a poem. Prose would have been bad enough but poetry produced panic and procrastination. Finally, at the last minute, his back against the wall, he wrote an amusing parody of "I must go down to the sea again." To his amazement the faculty thought it so good they required him to stand up and read it at the final assembly. The audience loved it and one parent came to him afterwards saying, "You certainly have a wonderful way with words." "Shot with luck, more like it," Andrew laughed to himself. His laugh is big, deep, and frequent.

Everything about Andrew is big. He seems to overflow most rooms. Walls seem inappropriate and boundaries Lilliputian. When his Graduate Record Exam scores came, for instance, he thought there had been an error because he received 812, although the published perfect score is 800. The score was correct, explained the testing service. They expect everyone to make one or two mistakes so they call 800 perfect. Actually it is possible, though very rare, to score over that number.

Andrew has always had a gigantic supply of physical energy. Throughout his youth he ran, batted, bounced, kicked, dove, chinned, and played team sports and individual sports with equal energy and enthusiasm.

He strides toward challenge in seven-league boots, taking issues seriously but seldom himself. He has not been burdened by hiding and hurting. In a naive, unself-conscious way he has not yet realized how extraordinary he is.

As he moves from business school, where quick, aggressive thinking is acceptable, to real-life business situations in which tact and political reality may require the youngest, most junior team player to hide his light under a bushel, he meets a dilemma. He must discover how to use his brain, and what it generates, without mowing down other people. Having finally decided to choose

173

business over architecture, he must find ways to satisfy his enormous aesthetic appetite. These present two hefty challenges to his problem-solving ability!

When asked his three wishes he laughed, put his arm around the diminutive law school student with whom he has lived for the past five years, and said, "The first thing would be a rich girl friend!" Then, turning uncharacteristically shy, he said he'd like to be able to speak three or four other languages. After that he thought and said, "I don't really have a whole lot of wishes. If I want something I guess I just go out and do it if it matters to me. That sounds arrogant—I don't mean it to. I guess I just trust in my own strength. Oh, here's one: I'd like to do reasonably well in the Boston Marathon. I don't want to win it—I don't want to spend that much time working out, but I'd like to just go in cold, and do reasonably well."

Stephen, Age 25

Stephen comes from a family in which aesthetic sensitivity and intellectual achievement are highly valued. Their life and his schooling reflect these priorities. As a young child his scholastic achievement was superior in all respects. He knew things other children had never heard of, he saw connections other people missed, and he has always been highly articulate. He is now a professional musician. He sings and is the director of a new, exciting opera workshop. He said, "I was relieved to settle on music. I can't 'con' music. I was so used to bullshitting my way through everything else. I always got A's but I wasn't doing anything. You can't get away with that in singing."

Stephen's dilemma, which music resolved for him, was how to stay intellectually honest when he continually received high grades for work he knew was superficial. Cynicism is frequently

174

born of undeserved praise and effortless success. Stephen has given himself, completely, to the discipline of his art and finds joy in its rigor. In addition to singing and directing, he writes. He was an editor of *Opera News Magazine*, to which he contributed regularly. He assembled programs and materials for teachers to use in regular classrooms, and in cooperation with the Metropolitan Opera is writing a book for young people. He wants so much to share his perceptions, bursting the dowager-like balloon of pomposity many people associate with opera, and bringing it close to an audience and age group traditionally antagonistic.

From early childhood an obligation to share and teach has accompanied his awareness of his own gifts. In his own words, "I need to make public the insane passion I have for opera and all that it can be."

Stephen's three wishes:

to be able to communicate the full joy of the things with which I'm gifted;

to have enough money to be able to stay tan all year;

to end up doing what uses my talents, is fulfilling, and gives me the spectrum of excitement I need as a person.

Talbert, Age 47

Controversial, articulate, in love with challenge and surprise, Talbert is finding personal fulfillment after resigning from a job which was a pinnacle of worldly success. Academic honors and positions of leadership have always been his. It seems that he needed to accumulate them in order to flesh out a required personal and family portrait. Then, having done so, he needed to discard their trappings in order to commit himself completely to his own life and to realize his particular potential. So many times

175

successful people become prisoners of their own positions. Fear of losing supremacy leads to a timidity and rigidity which contradict the qualities behind the original success. Talbert has not been netted.

His early scholastic performance in no way predicted his subsequent brilliance. From first through fourth grade he had little idea what he was meant to be doing or what schooling was supposed to accomplish. For example, he remembers sitting in an arithmetic lesson in a prestigious New York City boy's school doing an addition problem made up of several rows of five-digit numbers. To his eye they made a beautiful design. With no regard for mathematical process he enthusiastically invented some glamorous-looking totals. His teacher, in exasperation, showed the paper to the headmaster, who interpreted it as final evidence that Talbert should pursue learning somewhere else.

So it was he found himself headed off to boarding school to repeat the fourth grade. He was there for five years, joyously throwing himself into the artistic and athletic as well as the academic life of the school. Participating in their work program, he discovered for the first time how much he liked being the foreman. He not only enjoyed being in control, but learned very early that a boss's dedication to a job is usually far greater than other people's, and therefore realistic expectations must be set accordingly. He learned this lesson young and has never forgotten it. He loved the freedom of earning his wage and spending it as he wished at the local bubble gum emporium. Looking back on those years, he describes the warmth, structure, and opportunity for artistic expression of a school which helped many troubled and gifted students.

Having deservedly won a reputation for intellectual prowess, Talbert went to a large boarding school that offered more freedom than he could handle. When he was expelled his father was furious: "steely and cold." He was accepted at another boarding school whose headmaster saw promise in the boy. Once there, he lived as much as possible on his own resources, consciously separating himself from the other students. He felt different from them and wanted to show it. His years there were marked by solitude but not loneliness and provided the external discipline he needed. Of course his pride required him to fight the rules. He accomplished this not by shirking his studies but by devouring them. Since dormitory lights, controlled by a master switch, were extinguished at an hour deemed suitable for growing boys, Talbert bribed the maid for a key to her room where he would go after lights out to study late and illegally.

He went to college and after some recurrent difficulty in handling freedom, discovered his area of intellectual passion quite by chance in a course he took to balance his degree requirements. From the first lecture he was hooked. After graduating summa cum laude, he continued through graduate school and at the age of twenty-eight was filled with knowledge, vigor, and sharp memory of what it was like to be the foreman.

He became foreman many times in the ensuing twenty years, each time being known as the youngest, most audacious, and frequently most controversial person to have held each of the varying positions. But the more renowned the organizations he headed, the more restricted Talbert felt. It seems that his period of hiding and hurting came simultaneously with high visibility and professional acclaim.

Several years ago he resigned from a secure, rather glamorous position, leaving himself with no salary and an unknown future. Today he says that was one of the best decisions he has ever made. He has started his own enterprise and finally has found something which can absorb all that bubbles up from within him. He is alive, awake, and filled with zest. Once again, he is the foreman, but this time there are no restrictions of tradition and no limits to scope. He seems to have outgrown his need for externally imposed discipline and to be ready to manage the obligations of freedom. Of his wishes Talbert says:

I wish that the joy I have in writing really translates into professionalism.
I wish that someday I could really tell the truth.
I wish that I may never lose the sense of controversy.

Pamela, Age 51

Pamela describes herself as "a scientist turned generalist." She was born abroad and came to this country at the age of three when her father, a distinguished scientist and professor, was appointed department chairman at an outstanding American university. She says her mother and father always assumed that their only child would be a gifted student and a high achiever. They wanted to identify with democratic American practice and ideals; consequently they sent their daughter to the public school near the university. Schoolwork came easily to Pamela and she accelerated, completing the eighth grade when she was only eleven. The plan for her to return to England for further schooling was changed by World War II. She recrossed the ocean and ended up adoring the sociability of her Canadian boarding school from which she graduated in glory. She entered Radcliffe as a sophomore at age sixteen. She went from Radcliffe to MIT and by the age of twenty-three had earned her Ph.D. She laughs now and says it seemed easier to get a Ph.D. than to learn to type. She continued her scientific work in the early years of her marriage and, having given birth to three children, changed from science to independent education, which offered her an opportunity to have the same hours and calendar year as her children. She became headmistress and served in that capacity for thirteen years. From there she went to be head of a

178

national organization devoted to young people, and was the first woman elected to the board of directors of two major corporations. Later, for a brief period, she was president of a company working on energy problems. In retrospect she says she never felt like a driven career woman. Rather she thinks she always took the path of least resistance.

At fifty-one she is looking for her next path. She is no longer married and her children are independent. She says she adores playing with ideas. She leans toward science, saying, "A scientist is a creative entrepreneur." Her interests are widespread and she has many theoretical options open to her. She enjoys playing with the question of choices—who has them? How many are real, how many mirage?

Pamela's is different from the classic mid-life dilemma of a woman trying to decide what to do next. Her intellectual capacity must be used and her previous level of achievement matched. Not for her the reentry-level job in sportswear at Lord and Taylor. What is the next thing this generalist will generate?

Pamela wishes:

to have contributed ideas to society and have them put into action;

to see her children find inner peace and emotional as well as intellectual satisfaction through wise and careful choice of lifelong partners;

to follow their example and do the same.

Linda, Age 54

Linda grew up in the outskirts of a large midwestern industrial city. She received her education in a nationally famous public school system, where she was an outstanding student in science, mathematics, foreign languages, and English, including both literary criticism and composition. She was raised by a divorced mother and had one sister, much older than she, who became an alcoholic. Linda attended a university near her home where she continued to be an outstanding student, graduating summa cum laude. Her thesis on interactions of poetry and philosophy in eighteenth-century England was published and received favorable reviews. Although she majored in English literature, she continued her studies in mathematics and history.

After graduating from college, Linda took a job with a publishing company. She stayed there for six years, finally leaving because she felt restricted. She changed to a job which offered opportunities for scientific research. She enjoyed it initially, but soon outgrew it. Her mother died, and her sister was frequently hospitalized for alcoholism.

Linda moved to California where she took a job teaching history and English to high school students. She enrolled in a doctoral program at a nearby university. After several years, she lost her enthusiasm for teaching and decided to pursue her studies full time. She married a wealthy man who longed for her companionship. They had not known each other well before the marriage, and they subsequently proved incompatible. Their passionless divorce left Linda financially secure for the first time in her life.

That was eleven years ago. Linda never finished her doctoral work. She has volunteered in some political campaigns and helped out with a few ecological projects. She tried her hand at writing, and has published two articles in a local newspaper. She has acquired a small white dog and rents an attractive house.

She wishes:

to have a garden without weeds;
to have E.S.P.;
to go into space.

Jean, Age 75

Jean was the oldest in a family of seven children born to a successful industrialist and his southern wife. She contracted poliomyelitis in her girlhood and was crippled as a result. Walking required supreme effort and her hands were badly twisted. After graduating from school with highest academic honors, she tried to adjust to her family's expectations that she would be content to stay at home, but she could not. She was sensitive and scientifically gifted with wide-ranging curiosity and an imperative need to experience life. Tea on the terrace, lovely and warm though it was, did not fill her up. In her late twenties she went to Barnard College, where she was an unusual student. Her age and her physical disability made her noticeable. So did the outstanding quality of her work. (The story of her being accepted at Barnard is in Chapter Four.)

To the astonishment of her family, she applied and was admitted to the College of Physicians and Surgeons of Columbia University. She finished medical school and completed a residency, not shirking any duties. She rode the ambulances and climbed staircases in tenement buildings alongside her classmates in spite of the physical difficulties these jobs presented. Then she was trained to be a psychoanalyst. She had an active psychiatric practice in New York City for more than twenty-five years, working well into her seventies.

A common bond among her many dilemmas was forged by her need to make peace between two very different sides of her own nature: the gentle, reflective, domestic side, and the intellectually aggressive, scientific, inquisitive side. She had to first acknowledge and then channel her powerful drives when she realized she could not spend her life docilely at home. In order to be the gracious young woman her mother's southern tradition and contemporary custom required, she had to conceal the quickness

181

and power of her mind. Once again, a gifted person was hiding and hurting.

After her career decisions had been made and she had begun her studies and work, it was difficult to maintain warm, strong relationships with some of her relatives and family friends. In spite of being proud of her determination and success, some did not understand her need to be independent, and others were surprised and shocked by the branch of medicine she chose. In the 1940s many people considered psychiatry unscientific and unclean. She faced further dilemmas of studying and working while shackled by severe physical limitations and the difficulties of moving ahead in her profession, being disabled, a woman, and single.

Tapping her deepest reservoirs of will power and warmth, she was able to separate her professional life from her life as a willing member of a large, extended family with powerful traditions and taboos. She learned how to be the receiver of human nature's darkest secrets during the day, and in the evening, a gracious Southern hostess, appreciative of assistance, sharing in gentle desultory conversation. She made those around her—little children, awkward adolescents, tired young mothers, the middle-aged and the elderly—feel warm, interesting, and capable. Thoughtless people referred to her as sweet. She was not sweet.

She preserved her gentle, empathetic, generous qualities by stubbornly refusing to let bitterness taint them. This was a monumental task, requiring perpetual vigilance. She tempered the steel of her spirit with intellect, energy, and determination. She managed thus to convert her anguish for the things she could not have (a husband, children, physical well-being) into profound understanding of others' needs and fears.

She wished:

to figure skate;

to know all Shakespeare's plays by heart without ever having to
    memorize them;
not to need to waste the long night hours in sleep.

She died in 1976. Virginia Woolf wrote a tribute to George
Eliot, another gifted woman who struggled against both physical
weakness and the prejudice of her society against women writers.
It is a fitting epitaph for Jean.

For her too the burden and complexity of womanhood were not
enough; she must reach beyond the sanctuary and pluck for herself the
strange bright fruits of art and knowledge. Clasping them as few women
have ever clasped them, she would not renounce her own inheritance—
the difference of view, the difference of standard—not accept an inappropriate reward . . . reaching out with "a fastidious yet hungry ambition" for all that life could offer the free and inquiring mind, and con-
fronting her feminine aspirations with the real world of men. Trium-
phant was the issue for her, whatever it may have been for her creations,
and as we recollect all that she dared and achieved, how with every obstacle against her—sex and health and convention—she sought more
knowledge and more freedom till the body, weighted with its double
burden, sank worn out, we must lay upon her grave whatever we have it
in our power to bestow of laurel and rose.[1]

[1]Virginia Woolf, *The Common Reader* (New York, Harcourt Brace Jovanovich,
Inc., 1955), p. 176.

Epilogue

Treat gifted children as real people. Look into their eyes as well as their IQs. They are not freaks unless we make them so.

Help them develop powerful bonds to their world and other people. Do not separate them from humanity, join them to it.

Nurture them with honesty, humor, and common sense that they may grow into whole people and, bright to brilliant, shine among us.

P. L.V.
August 1978

Appendix

1. A Book

The papers presented at the first World Conference on Gifted Children, which was held in London in September 1975, are collected in *Gifted Children, Looking to Their Future,* Edited by Joy Gibson and Prue Chennells, published in 1976 by Latimer New Dimensions Ltd., 14 West Central Street, London WCIAI JH, England.

2. Some Organizations

AMERICAN ASSOCIATION FOR GIFTED CHILDREN
15 Gramercy Park South
New York, N. Y. 10003
Marjorie Craig, Executive Director

COUNCIL OF STATE DIRECTORS OF PROGRAMS FOR GIFTED
California State Department of Education
721 Capital Mall
Sacramento, California 95814
Paul D. Plowman, President

187

ERIC Clearing House on G/T
Council for Exceptional Children
1920 Association Drive
Reston, Va. 22091

METROPOLITAN COUNCIL FOR GIFTED
40 Seventh Avenue South
New York, N.Y. 10014
Virginia Z. Ehrlich, President

NATIONAL ASSOCIATION FOR GIFTED CHILDREN
8080 Springvalley Drive
Cincinnati, Ohio 45236
John Curtis Gowan, President

THE NATIONAL ASSOCIATION FOR GIFTED CHILDREN
1 S. Audley Street
London W1Y 5DA, England
Henry Collis, Director

THE NATIONAL ASSOCIATION OF INDEPENDENT
SCHOOLS
4 Liberty Square
Boston, Massachusetts

OFFICE OF GIFTED AND TALENTED EDUCATION
U.S. Office of Education
Room 2100, ROB-3, 7th and D Streets, S.W.
Washington, D.C. 20202
Director, Harold Lyon; Deputy Director, Jane Case Williams

THE ASSOCIATION FOR THE GIFTED (TAG)
A division of the Council for Exceptional Children
1411 South Jefferson Davis Highway
Arlington, Virginia 22202
Joseph Renzulli, President

3. Some Publications

THE GIFTED CHILD QUARTERLY
Route 5, P.O. Box 630A
Hot Springs, Arkansas 71901
This is available to members of the National Association for
Gifted Children.

THE ROEPER REVIEW: A Journal on Gifted Child Education
2190 N. Woodward Avenue
Bloomfield Hills, Michigan 48013

4. Some Publishers

CREATIVE PUBLICATIONS
P.O. Box 10328
Palo Alto, California 94303

DOVER PUBLICATIONS
180 Varick Street
New York, N.Y. 10014

DRAKE HOME CRAFTSMEN'S BOOKS
801 Second Avenue
New York, N.Y. 10017

GOLDEN PRESS PUBLISHERS
850 Third Avenue
New York, N.Y. 10022

McCALLS
230 Park Avenue
New York, N.Y. 10017

SCHOLASTIC MAGAZINES AND BOOK SERVICES
906 Sylvan Avenue
Engelwood Cliffs, N.J. 07632

189

SUNSET HOBBY AND CRAFT BOOKS
Lane Publishing Co.
Menlo Park, California 94025

TIME/LIFE BOOKS
1271 Avenue of the Americas
New York, N.Y. 10020

WALKER AND CO.
720 Fifth Avenue
New York, N.Y. 10019

5. Simulation Game

Here is some further information on the simulation game described briefly in Chapter Seven. To contact the originator write to:

Mr. John P. Fennell
Head of the Middle School
The Rippowam-Cisqua School
Bedford, New York 10506

Reprinted here, with Mr. Fennell's permission, are a sample ritual and myth for each of his three tribes.

SPIRITUAL RITUAL OF THE MAMAZONS

Each year, at the end of the rainy season, the Mamazons make their annual pilgrimage to Mama, a sacred volcanic mountain located at the very heart of their territory. To reach this high place of worship, the Mamazons must first traverse the Great Falls, whose thundering roar and violent spume make the swaying, cantilevered, vine supported cat-walks seem fragile indeed. Arriving at the foot of Mana, the younger and stronger of the venerable Clan-Mother's husbands secure her firmly to a bamboo lifter and, hoisting her carefully on their broad shoulders, begin the long, treacherous assent over the jagged lava flows to the summit. In accordance with long-standing tradition the Clan-Mother is followed in solemn procession by blood relatives: mothers and daughters in the lead, husbands and sons trailing respectfully behind. Upon reaching the summit, the members of the tribe arrange themselves along the lip of the volcanic opening and begin the Flame Dance, a strictly prescribed series of undulating body movements which slowly gather in intensity as the drums increase in tempo. By nightfall the fires have been lit and the dancers are nearing frenzy. Six male infants, born within the last year, are brought forth and prepared for the sacrifice. Chanting sacred incantations, the She-Doctor smears the tiny bodies with berry juice and snake oil. Finally, as the dancers moan and cry out in exhausted euphoria, the six infants are fed to the waiting mouth of Mama; for a time the smouldering and ravenous force within shall be propitiated.

MAMAZON MYTH

Mama is all powerful, the great force that occupies the land and water and sky. Mama can bring good luck to peoples, and she who possesses more of Mama shall be the She-Doctor. Mama can also bring bad luck. Mama can become very angry. When Mama is angry the whole earth shakes. Mama can destroy all. Mama can bury all. Mama can burn all. Mama can swallow all. Mama is always hungry. Mama is always seething. Mama's energy is always there, ready to burst forth. Mama must be respected above all. Mama must be fed and chanted to. If Mama is not happy, Mama will bring bad, bad luck. May Mama never be unhappy.

APPENDIX

SPIRITUAL BELIEFS AND RITUAL OF THE VORICHIS

The Vorichis believe in one great spirit, Puritani Vorichi. Upon coming of age, each Vorichi is initiated into the society by receiving a wooden disk, cut from a sacred tomarand or hemlock, the grain and markings of which indicate his life path, his fate— everything from his mate to his material success.

Four times a year they hold gigantic feasts. All Vorichis gather and bring the best of their flocks. They are seated in concentric circles around a large wooden totem, with those who bring more woven blakets, dried scrod, and wild corn forming the Inner Circle. Everyone partakes and sacrifices, with the Inner Circle chanting a prayer vouching for the diligent work which the tribe has performed.

VORICHI MYTH

And Puritani looked with favor upon the Vorichis and he multiplied their flocks and the food of the sea. And each Vorichi waxed great in his goods for the toil he undertook, so that none was withdrawn from the Inner Circle, but all had grace and favor.

And it came to pass that the old Vorichis became lax and forgot Puritani's commands. They no longer labored but spoke to one another, saying, "Why should we toil when slight effort increases our goods hundredfold?" They took after vanity, forgetting the sacred feasts.

Puritani became exceedingly angry and hid his face from the Vorichis. "Thou has not called upon me, O Vorichis, nor wearied yourselves for me. Nor hast thou honored me with thy paintings and carvings." In his wrath he turned to the Warlike Ones and caused them to wax mighty.

Therefore the Warlike Ones swept as the raging blizzard from the North. As a shark within a net did they destroy all in their path,

192

burning cabins and boats alike. The remnant of the tribe of Vorichi fled to the forests, each family unto itself.

And the remnant saw the smoking, barren ruins that had been their home and portion. Our fathers were ashamed and knew that they had done evil. They worked and seated, and Puritani forgave them, setting them apart from their ancestors by calling them the New Vorichi.

Hence, it has been from that time forth, that Puritani has looked with favor upon those that toil and gives sustenance for their labor, but withholds his hand from those that seek to ease their burdens and casts them to the outermost circle. It is for us of the New Vorichi to abide by his command, lest we are again afflicted by the Warlike Ones.

SIGNIFICANT URBANIAN CEREMONIES

Urbanian religious life is organized by the High Priests around ceremonies of various types and importance. Just before the swelling of the Great River, the High Priests have spent many evenings on the tall walls of the city calculating the precise moment when the ceremony should begin.

Accompanied by a vicious guard dog, younger less important Priests have already collected assorted grains, stoneware, and jewelry from the lesser classes, for use in the Harvest Ceremony. Most of this tax is laid at the foot of the Golden Statue of the Great Dog God, while the remainder goes to satisfy lesser deities.

Smaller ceremonies are held whenever necessary to divine and assure the success of Urbanian conquests in foreign lands. The Emperor picks from all the guard dogs the one he deems the most strong and fierce. The High Priests then administer a secret sleeping potion, lay the unconscious dog upon a layer of carefully leveled, red river mud, and cut it open. The Emperor, in a trance, makes his interpretation from the dog's entrails and the cracks in the now dried mud. He assigns his Generals to their tasks and retreats once again into the Temple.

URBANIAN MYTH

There was once a very old priest who chanted the first coming of the Great Dog God. His story, long since put down in clay by the High Priests, told of a red tinge, shaped like a dog's face, surrounding the bright cross in the evening sky. The very next day at dusk there appeared a brown and black dog—as tall as the combined height of two men—who ended the conquest by invaders seeking the rich farming soil of Urbania. Ever since that day the people, who live in this land fringed by yellow sand, have been in awe of their Emperor, who has in him the blood of the Great Dog God.

In more recent years, however, the Emperor has grown listless and full of worry; his guard dogs have dwindled in number and the Emperor feels that the lower classes will soon try to take over his Palace. He prays nightly to the Great Dog God to help him find more dogs with which to protect his palace and his priests.

The Emperor is also bothered terribly by the fact that the High Priests have not yet been able to choose a suitable heir to his kingdom from all the sons of his many fair wives. The son who seems to be the most capable warrior and teller of the future will follow in his father's footsteps as the next blood descendent of the fearless Dog God.

Index

195

INDEX

196

INDEX

197

INDEX

198

INDEX

199

INDEX

INDEX

201

INDEX